ONE MORE BEER, PLEASE

Q&A With American Breweries Vol. 2

JON NELSEN

LifeLevelUpBooks.com

One More Beer, Please

Q&A With American Breweries

Vol. 2

Published by **LIFE LEVEL UP**

King of Prussia, PENNSYLVANIA, U.S.A.

Jon Nelsen, Author

One More Beer, Please

Q&A With American Breweries

Vol. 2

Jon Nelsen

QUANTITY PURCHASES: Schools, companies, professional groups, clubs,

and other organizations may qualify for special terms when ordering quantities of this title.

For information, email sales@lifelevelupbooks.com.

Life Level Up

CONTENTS

INTRODUCTION

I think it's safe to say I am a craft beer fanatic. From the very first sip of craft beer, I knew it was something special.

This three book set resulted from lots of hard work, both for me and for the many many breweries who took the time to respond and answer my questions. I wrote this because like many of you I have a dream of one day opening a brewery I can call my own. Also like many of you, I have more questions than answers and this was my attempt to get as much of a peak behind the curtain of American craft beer as the breweries would allow.

I asked simple open-ended questions and the variety of answers I received make these books some of the most informative on the subject of American Craft Beer. I received responses from national breweries to small breweries in a shed. Answers from homebrewers turned pro, to college educated brew masters and everyone in between. In fact, I even received answers from Abbey Monks brewing to support their real mission of ministry. Best of all, it wasn't just brewers who answered me back. I heard from owners, bartenders, marketers, and even spouses.

Some breweries had just opened, some had just closed, and some have been going strong for decades with no end in sight. This book was written during the height of the 2020 covid crisis and while it was alluded to in some responses, most of the breweries made the choice to focus on the bright future of craft beer rather than the doom and gloom of the present. I want to thank all the great American breweries who helped me compile these books and took the time out of their busy schedules to allow me to share their thoughts with the world.

Breweries provide places to relax and escape everyday life, opportunities to see old friends and meet new ones, a place to bond over a shared love of the better things in life, and taste something that is only limited by creativity of the one crafting it. Craft beer in America provides jobs in almost every town and support to the communities they serve. Every brewery has a story to share and I hope you will not only listen to what they say, but support the breweries who are facing a constant battle to provide the highest quality product when it seems quality is forsaken for cheap and boring.

I hope you enjoy reading this as much as I enjoyed putting it together. Each book contains discussions with at least 100 breweries and endless insight into their thoughts, strategies, preferences, product development and history. I tried to leave their thoughts and words as they put them and preferred authenticity rather than highly edited responses. Please be sure to grab a copy of all 3 books as each one contains some interviews that I thought were truly mind-blowing. The responses you see on these pages are exactly how they wrote it, and with no major. The exception being editing a few swear words and references to big beer companies. So grab a beer and enjoy the opportunity to learn from some of the best in the business.

Jon Nelsen

IF YOU LOVE CRAFT BEER:
lifelevelupbooks.com/beer

Drink Local and Drink Often

Q&A WITH OVER 300 AMERICAN BREWERIES

EARTH BREAD + BREWERY

7136 Germantown Ave
Philadelphia, PA 19119

Peggy Zwerver
Owner

What year did you open and typically, how much beer do you guys make in a year?

Opened 10/2008. We produce about 160bbls per year

How much beer do you personally consume on an average workday?

I don't know if you want to use us for this one.....we mostly drink wine these days. But Tom, since he's the brewer, tries a couple of the beers each day

What's your favorite food to eat with beer and why?

I think Indian food and IPA go great together

About how much does it cost to open a brewery?

Kind of arbitrary…..how big is your brewhouse….how big is the pub. It cost us about $300k in 2008

In your opinion, if you were opening a brewery today what is the best BBL size to start with and why?

We like the 7bbl that we have. We usually have guest drafts on as well. So there's more variety.

When you first opened the brewery, what was the biggest obstacle? What advice would you give someone thinking about opening a brewery to avoid some pitfalls you experienced?

Breweries are different than brewpubs. Staffing is always challenging. And train that staff. My advice is to shadow a current owner. See what their day to day is like

What separates breweries that don't make it in this business from the ones that do?

Good beer. Not everyone can brew good beer.

How did you first discover craft beer and what made you want to enter the business?

My husband and I were in IT (analysts, programmers) and were burnt out. He took that opportunity to go to brewing school and turn a hobby into a career.

What beer would you brew if cost, production, and sales were no object?

We don't restrict ourselves that way. It would be nice to use local malt but often the price is too high

Do you think a new brewery should serve food or just beer?

Whatever you do – do it right. Don't do it just to do it.

What beer is your brewery best known for and why?

Unusual styles. Tom loves to brew fruits, sours, goze

End of a long brew day, what are you drinking?

Atlbier

ELM STREET BREWING CO.

519 N. Elm St.
Muncie, IN 47305

Seth Ruskowsky
Head Brewer

Typically, how much beer do you guys produce in an average year?

Typically we're right around the 300-350 Barrel mark, which would be about 600-700 half barrel (15.5 gal) kegs a year

How much beer do you personally consume on an average workday?

Typically, I drink less than one beer during the average work day. The only time I drink during the work day is pulling samples from a fermenter or brite tank to see where the beer is at. Usually these samples are less than 2 ounces a peice, and at the most I'll drink 5 samples a day, however that almost never happens. I know of some brewers that drink during their brewdays, but I guess I just treat this a little more seriously. After work, I will sometimes drink a shift beer, but even that isn't every day.

What's your favorite food to eat with beer and why?

I may be one of the weird ones, but I don't typically drink with food. I know the whole food pairing idea is a thing, and I've tried many of the "traditional" food pairings and it's never really done anything for me. Again, I am probably the weird one.

About how much does it cost to open a brewery?

I think a lot of the cost depends on the size, location and business model of the brewery. If you're trying to make a production brewery, you're spending more money on brewing equipment, cold boxes, cans/canners etc, but if you're on a tap room model like ourselves, you need to jam a lot of money into that tap room to attract people to your location and to your beer. I think at the bare minimum you could get away with scraping something together for $100,000ish, but that's going to be bare bones, little to no taproom and only an employee or two.

Do you think a new brewery should serve food or just beer?

Legally, you have to have some sort of food available, however there are creative ways around that. I have a unique perspective to this question, because the first year we were open we didn't do food, and for the past two years we have. If it was my choice, if I was planning to open a brewery myself, I would not have a full kitchen. The kitchen helps, because people are willing to stay longer if there's food involved, but your margins on food aren't typically that great. Our current Friday nights (before the pandemic) we were averaging with food, what our best night without food was, however, that night before food was more profitable because the margins on beer are so massive.

In your opinion, if you were opening a brewery today what is the best BBL size to start with and why?

If I were to open a brewery today, I would probably grab a 5-7bbl system. I currently brew on a 5bbl and it's a really nice size, I think I would just like those extra 2 bbls because it would be a little easier to distribute more. The benefit of something smaller like that, is you can always get a 10 or 15 bbl fermenter and double batch into it, but it's a bit harder to do a half batch of anything if you had a 15 bbl brewhouse.

What are today's worst beer trends?

Unfermented fruit juice in beers that cause cans to explode, inaccurate ABVs, and IP Theft.

What separates breweries that don't make it in this business from the ones that do?

The liquid! You don't go out of business if you make good beer (Unless you also make bad business decisions). There's breweries in the middle of nowhere that have no problem, and there's breweries in the middle of huge cities struggling. Your marketing can be crap, your tap room can be a hole in the wall, but none of that matters if your beer is good.

In the past few years we have seen a massive surge in the popularity of Hazy IPA's and Sours, what do you believe the next popular beer style will be?

I think IPAs and sours are here to stay for a long time. In our market, IPAs have been king for all 12 years I've been in the industry. I think there's something to be said about Hard Seltzers, and I think a lot of people will be doing lighter lagers and session ales to try and bring drinkers back from Hard Seltzer into beer.

When you first opened the brewery, what was the biggest obstacle? What advice would you give someone thinking about opening a brewery to avoid some of the pitfalls you experienced?

Our biggest obstacles all had to deal with the local government. We were lucky enough that one of the owners was a national contractor and knew everything building commissioners and fire marshals were going to inspect. However, dealing with small town bureaucracy isn't for the faint of heart!

What beers are you best known for and why?

In the grand scheme of things, we're relatively unknown. We're probably in the bottom 20% of breweries in Indiana when it comes to size, so people away from our area don't necessarily know of us. Our customers know us for our IPAs and innovative sours, beer geeks who may not come here often, but have seen us at beerfests have had mostly our sours and IPAs. Here's one of the random ones I head from people: we did a collaboration with another brewery and did a Ketchup Gose... probably one of the weirder beers we've done. It had no reason to be as good as it was.

What sets your brewery apart from most others?

In our small area, our taproom looks unlike anything else in this area. We're in the Muncie Ice House built in the 1890s, very industrial, large, and well put together. We also have a huge patio/outdoor area. We still hear this almost 4 years in "Wow, this doesn't feel like Muncie"- we love Muncie, but that was kind of the point! From the beer perspective, we brew a lot of strange and experimental beers, especially for the area.

How do you decide on new beers to brew?

As the head brewer, thankfully it's completely up to me! I've been in the industry for 12 years, and have always kept up on trends and styles. I try to keep our beers as relevant as I can. Sometimes I have a beer and think "I wonder how they did that" and think about it for weeks before writing a recipe. Other times I wake up in the middle of the night with an idea, write it down and maybe I'll brew it that week or in a year. One of the last beers I put out, a cucumber melon mint sour was on my list for about 8 months before I got to it.

What are the biggest reasons for the continual growth of craft breweries?

I think there's a lot of people that like the idea of supporting local. Craft Beer is more of a commodity, and the people that are willing to spend $6 a pint (when they can get a 6pk of domestics for the same price) like to try and keep their money in their local economy. Also, I think social media gives a lot of people fear of missing out.

What are the biggest obstacles to continued craft beer growth?

I think the biggest obstacles are poorly run business or poorly made beer. If I'm new to craft beer and buy a $5 pint and it sucks, maybe I just think this stuff isn't for me. Just because you made 5 loaves of bread at home, doesn't mean you should start a bakery, but there's a lot of people who homebrew a few batches and decide to open their own spot.

Bigger, more established breweries who are releasing unfinished product that can explode, or product with a false ABV makes people think that it's widespread in the industry. "Why would I trust this new, small taproom when the big guys have been caught lying?" It hurts all of us.

What are the biggest problems you run into in producing beer?

Ingredient availability. There's many types of hops that I would use all year, except when they go on sale, they're expensive and quickly sell out. There's many different adjuncts, fruit or even vanilla that I would like to use, but either these items are not available, or cost an arm and a leg.

How do you reach beyond the hardcore beer drinkers and into the general public to sell your beer?

I think the biggest benefit of having a full kitchen with your taproom is just this. I don't have to reach out to the general public to sell my beer, because the public packs out our taproom every weekend, and need to drink something. The benefit of having most (Like 95%) of our beer going through our taproom, is that when I do have the time or product to distribute I can choose where it goes without really having to sell it. Typically, the best way to get your name known by the general public is doing Beerfests as often as you can.

How did you first discover craft beer and what made you want to enter the business?

I needed a college job, and had a few friends working at a bottle shop about a block away from where I lived. I thought it would be fun working with friends, and being in a college town, I thought I would see a lot of people my age in the store. That specific location had over 500 different craft beers and I started learning about them strictly out of necessity first. After a few years of talking craft beer and reading, you start getting more and more into it, soon I realized I was going to be in this industry for the rest of my life.

How do you attempt to increase beer production while still staying true to both your brand and your unique styles?

The only way for us to increase production is to completely expand the brewing area and adding more fermenters. I don't think you have to sacrifice your brand or styles to expand, but if you go from a 5 bbl to a 50 bbl, sometimes the general public will see your brand differently. I don't know how many times I've heard "____ beer was so much better before they got big" I don't know if that's an accurate statement, or if it's a hipster-y "It was better before everyone knew about it".

What's the style most fun to brew?

I like brewing sours, the best. We kettle sour, so it breaks my brewday up a little. Instead of a 12-14 hour brewday, it may be 8 hours one day and 5 when I'm finishing it. Further, I think there's a lot of fun stuff people aren't doing with sours, ingredients people aren't using, etc. Since sours are typically a little lighter on the ABV, there's some flavors that can come through better than you can in other beers. I also think the sourness of the base beer can really switch the flavor profile of certain ingredients.

What beer would you brew if cost, production, and sales were no object?

I would do some fruited lagers, more sours and some big barrel aged stouts.

Is there a popular beer you make that you just don't really like but everyone else loves?

Our best seller, a cream ale, I almost never drink. I brew it every other week or so, and taste it throughout the process, but when it gets to the taproom, I often forget about it.

End of a long brew day, what are you drinking?

Water and lots of it. This summer for instance, the area I brew in will be about 110 degrees on those especially hot days, and I'm stuck in that room for at least 8 hours. If I do really feel like a beer after, it would probably be something a little lighter, maybe a sour or a session IPA.

What are a few beers that other brewers are making that you really find impressive?

Everything that Urban Artifact out of Cincinnati does blows my mind. 18th Street from Gary/Hammond IN does some really well done IPAs and their sour brand, Sour Note has recently put out some really good stuff, different beers. I just had my first two beers from Viking Artisan Ales out of Griffith, IN that were great, and Transient up in Michigan never puts out anything bad. I identify most closely with Burn Em Brewing in Michigan City, as they do a lot of wild experimental stuff that I love trying. Lastly, Bare Hands Brewing out of Granger, IN easily has the best IPAs in the state (Elm Street a second close :-D) All of these guys impress and more importantly inspire me with what they're putting out.

How do you feel the internet has changed the way the craft brewing industry operates?

The internet has made it super easy for a small operation like us to be able to advertise and let our customers know what we've been up to. We do different dinner specials every night and without the internet we wouldn't be able to get that information out. With the good, comes the bad though.

When coming out with a new brew, how much experimentation do you do before you say it's ready for production?

Not nearly as much as one would think. Over the three years we've been open, we've done over 100 different beers and only about 10 of them have been made before they hit our system. When we opened I was the assistant brewer and everything Tyler, the old head brewer, did came out great, it felt like we had lightning in a bottle! Since then I took over and took the things that we learned early on and kept rolling with them. I think in the over 100 batches I've done since his departure, I've dumped 3 batches. Out of those batches, none of them were because of an idea not working, it was poor execution on an existing house beer.

I don't have the benefit of having a pilot system to try some of these ideas out, so typically I do a lot of research leading up to a new beer, experimental or not. When using an ingredient we've never used or style we've never done, I will look through the many beer books I have and get as much advice as I can on that specific ingredient or style.

Lastly, I make sure to go light on the ingredients I know can be problematic: too much mint can turn into toothpaste, too much lavender turns soapy or too much coconut can get into the sun tan lotion territory. You can always add more of an ingredient, but can't really take it out. Having so much experience in the industry, I can think back to the beers I've had over the years that have had specific ingredients and what made them good or bad, then go from there.

What style of beer is your best seller and why do you think that is?

Our best seller is a Cream Ale, and it's because it's typically the lightest thing we offer. We don't carry domestics, so one of our few "house" beers is a cream ale that sort of resembles a domestic. It's a beer that would do nothing in distribution, but one that I brew at least twice a month typically.

Does glassware really make a difference?

I don't think you need a specific glass for each specific beer, I think a snifter or tulip glass is a good catch all. Smell is a huge part of taste, as is look. I'm not much of a complainer, however if I have the choice, I will never use a tumbler, and especially not a glass straight out of the freezer.

What's the real difference between a Porter and a Stout?

No one really knows! Typically, I think a porter should be slightly lighter in body than a stout, but that's not really a quantifiable characteristic. Some of my favorite porters almost slip into the black IPA category. For me, Founders Porter is what everyone should base porters on- its body is a little on the lighter side, and at the end there's a small hop punch. If I was told that beer was a stout, I would be disappointed, but I think it's an almost perfect porter.

How important is IBU when it comes to picking out a beer? Do customers need to pay attention to it?

We place a lot of importance on IBU in our tap room. We would love for customers to pay attention to IBU, but we also understand everyone isn't drinking beer the way WE may drink beer. When I drink a beer, I'm thinking about it, evaluating it, and trying to pick out familiar flavors, but sometimes you just want to have a beer and talk, not think about it. When we do flights for instance, we have a carrier that lines the pours left to right, so we order them from lowest to highest IBU. People typically just drink the beers left to right, regardless of what order we put them in, but we always order them by IBU. If you have my Triple IPA w/ Blood Orange at 103 IBU, then drink our 18IBU Hoppy Hefe you'll probably be disappointed with the Hefe. The whole idea is to give people the best experience possible, and by not taking into account IBUs, you're severely diminishing their experience.

ESSEX COUNTY BREWING CO

58 Pulaski St Bldg A
Peabody, MA 01960

Paul Donhauser

What year did you open and typically, how much beer do you guys make in a year?

2018; we haven't had a typical year but did about 150 barrels

How much beer do you personally consume on an average workday?

Me, about 4 pints; our customers about 150 pints a day when we're open

What's your favorite food to eat with beer and why?

Depends; IPA with a steak; kolsch with lobster in summer; imperial stout in winter with s peanut butter fudge Sunday

About how much does it cost to open a brewery?

Depends ; $500k for 2k SF tap room and 20 bbl capacity

In your opinion, if you were opening a brewery today what is the best BBL size to start with and why?

Depends , but let's assume you have a high quality differentiated product ; I'd say 10-15 bbl; with a smaller pilot system

When you first opened the brewery, what was the biggest obstacle? What advice would you give someone thinking about opening a brewery to avoid some pitfalls you experienced?

Time..,,,2x your capital estimate; get a flexible lease with ability to expand; insure you test your product in the market outside of friends and family

What separates breweries that don't make it in this business from the ones that do?

Either poor quality and/or differentiated beer; poor core values or motives; lack of reality and business acumen

How did you first discover craft beer and what made you want to enter the business?

1994; experiencing something my dad loved (local quality beer; growing up in Germany); recreating a similar experience here in our area

What beer would you brew if cost, production, and sales were no object?

We do it today ; we spare no cost on our pharmaceutical grade water treatment or our floor malted grains or our ingredients

Do you think a new brewery should serve food or just beer?

You need a food liasonship to get ppl to enjoy 2-3 beers, especially with higher ABVs

What beer is your brewery best known for and why?

Too many to list all because of high quality ingredients and processes; IPAs; stouts;kolsch;fruited saison;etc

End of a long brew day, what are you drinking

I start with a session or kolsch/Pilsner; then go to a pale ale or single ipa and finish with a double ipa or stout

EIGHT-FOOT BREWING

4417 SE 16th PL., Unit 11
Cape Coral, FL 33904

Roger Phelps
Owner/Influencer of Microbial Reproduction

About how much does it cost to open a brewery?

This is a question a lot of people ask and I think it is very relative to their concept and goals in opening a brewery. We opened a brewery because we are passionate about beer. We strive to produce the highest quality beer, educate our community about unique, historical, and less known-styles, and provide a community-centric location that helps improve the lives of those around us. That being said, I started as a homebrewer 12 years ago. Something that drew me to the craft was how in-depth you could get along with a strong community of innovative problem solvers. I really enjoyed the hands-on approach and crafting everything myself. So, for us, we did as much as we possibly could. I ended up learning drafting and engineering in order to submit plans for renovation. I did a lot of the renovation and finishing myself. I pieced together a brew system. We took a very hands-on approach and were able to open our doors with money that we had.

A lot of people see breweries as a way to make a lot of money. In turn, they spend a lot of money on opening a state-of-the-art brewery and taproom. Recently, it seems to be trending towards small-business, families opening smaller breweries similar to us. They've been passionate about beer for 10+ years and are getting to a point where they are able to open a brewery. I think the craft beer trend started with this, then a lot of investors saw a huge market and now we are getting back to passionate brewers opening breweries on smaller budgets. This is certainly a good thing, as there is more competition and, in general, the beer available is much better than it was event 3-5 years ago.

When you first opened the brewery, what was the biggest obstacle? What advice would you give someone thinking about opening a brewery to avoid some of the pitfalls you experienced?

I would say be prepared to pivot. Like our current situation, where we've had to pivot our business model from maxing out our on premises consumption in our taproom to packaged sales only, you have to be ready to accept the problem and move forward. We ran into countless issues. One of the first, the guy we hired to do our architectural and engineering drawings strung us along and never provided us anything that passed code. We had already spent money on him and didn't have more in the budget to hire someone. So, I ended up learning how to do architectural and engineering plans and get them through all of the reviewers.

During my research into opening a brewery, the one thing that stuck out the most to me was that you had to be committed to seeing it through to the end. There would be a lot of difficulties to over-come. So, if it meant mowing lawns for a year while you work to get open, so be it.

What beers are you best known for and why?

How do you decide on new beers to brew?

I'll answer these together as the go hand in hand. We opened with the idea of maxing out our taproom using a small system. This allows us to always rotate our taps. While we do bring some beer back, we are often brewing something different. I really enjoy doing research and developing recipes, especially recreating historic examples. Right now we have a Tmave' Pivo (dark Czech lager), English Brown (traditional pub style beer), table beer (using kveik), California Common, German Helles, Hefeweizen, Porter, India Pale Lager - brewer using Hazy IPA techniques with lager yeast (some lager yeast has shown to be a higher bio transformer than ale yeast), Obsucrus (dark barrel fermented mixed ferm), Henrietta (amber barrel fermented mixed ferm).

We typically have three different categories of beer to choose from; 1) Clean beer - anything brewed using traditional brewers yeast and confirms to a style. 2) Alt Beer - using atypical yeast and doesn't necessarily conform to a style. We do a lot of Brett and Kveik beers. 3) Mixed Fermentation - using a variety of yeast and bacteria. This is probably the style we are best known for. We utilize mixed cultures I've had going for 6 years now to ferment these beers. We then often blend and referment on fruit.

End of a long brew day, what are you drinking?

Right now, Helles. I love lagers. Especially this one.

ELKTON BREWING CO.

100 N 5th St
Elkton, VA 22827

Tristan Napotnik
Branding and Marketing

About how much does it cost to open a brewery?

This totally depends on the business model and what size operation is intended. Our plan has never been to get in the distribution game, so our model is for a small self sustained brewery. If you want our beer, you have to come to us for it. This model requires significantly less funding than a bigger craft brewery who plans on bottling and canning for mass distribution.

Do you think a new brewery should serve food or just beer?

There is no right or wrong answer here. However, it seems to make more sense to offer food if there are no great restaurant or food truck options near your brewery. In our experience, local restaurants are happy to work with us and offer food delivery. This symbiotic relationship is a great way to both support a fellow local business while at the same time giving hungry patrons an option that encourages them to stay in our space. And if they stay, they drink. This is good for everyone. Otherwise, serving your own food at your brewery is a great option as well. We didn't want to deal with the headache of a commercial kitchen build out, nor the requirements for food to alcohol sales ratios, etc...

What are today's worst beer trends?

Since when is the bitterest the best? It seems that some breweries have overemphasized bitterness. We like to balance our beers well without allowing the bitterness of even our IPAs to overwhelm the taste of the beer itself. Sure, a little bitter here and there is great, but we personally like more complexity in each beer. The flavor profile is very important to us, and overemphasized bitterness can often rob from that flavor profile. Along those lines, some craft breweries seem to have a heavy lean one way or another: e.g. lots of IPAs and few dark beers, or lots of dark and roasty beers and nothing light, etc... Our goal, which has definitely received outstanding public feedback, has always been to have a well balanced selection of beers for every drinker.

What separates breweries that don't make it in this business from the ones that do?

That's a tough one to answer. This is obviously subjective and opinion-based, and depends on a lot of factors, many of which are out of anyone's control. It seems that when great atmosphere is paired with great beer, success is imminent. If you go to a brewery for the first time and you love the space but the beer is disappointing or mediocre, you probably won't go back. Likewise, if the beer is great but the taproom is not a place you like to hang out, then you might not patronize as often as if the space's atmosphere were better. We have worked hard at pairing both great beer and great atmosphere. We call the combo "Atmosbeer."

What sets your brewery apart from most others?

We are completely family owned and operated. Our building was part of our family business back in the 1980's, and we've repurposed it for the brewery. As lifetime members of our community, we've put a tremendous amount of emphasis on having our brewery be locally relevant. But doing so in a way that also creates an alluring vibe for visitors from anywhere else. We hope to become a destination brewery. All of our beers are named after local stories, landmarks, etc... These names are great conversation starters for non-locals, and they offer an inviting familiarity to locals. In 1890, our building started as a grain mill right on the railroad tracks in the middle of the small town of Elkton, Virginia. The architecture of the space is gorgeous and preserved. Within our space, we have two bars, a few lounge areas, and general seating areas with tables. We frequently hear from patrons that they stayed longer than they intended to because they enjoyed our space so much.

How do you decide on new beers to brew?

Much of it is supply and demand. I'm sure most breweries have to approach it from the business side of things. But it isn't ALL based on sales. There has to also be an element of fun and creativity. This is where our brewers, August Napotnik and Aaron Napotnik (my oldest brother and my youngest brother) have fun. This is where any craft brewer has fun. Take a standard recipe for a beer style and tweak it to accomplish a unique flavor profile. That's what August and Aaron do in our brew cellar every week.

What are the biggest reasons for the continual growth of craft breweries?

Atmosbeer! People love *good* beer. Emphasis on the word, "good." And people generally love community. Craft breweries have become social gathering places that are unique from restaurants, coffee shops, and sports bars, in that the space is much more fluid. People walk around, settle in one spot and then move to another, meet new people, etc... People are drawn to fellowship. What better way to share in fellowship than to gather for a pint or two? Or three.

How do you reach beyond the hardcore beer drinkers and into the general public to sell your beer?

Atmosbeer again! We've received a lot of great feedback from people who aren't "beer drinkers." When the atmosphere is inviting, unique, comfortable, fun, AND the beer selection has at least one beer for the light or non-beer drinker, that will create an experience they will want to return for. Social media is also helpful here. We can promote all we want, but ultimately the general public is our most effective influencer. The goal is to keep them our ally, because the general public's opinion really matters.

How did you first discover craft beer and what made you want to enter the business?

Our head brewer, August Napotnik, my oldest brother, started home-brewing in 2007. But the first Napotniks who came over from Austria in the early 1900's were old-school brewers too. Maybe it is in our family's blood. Co-brewer, Aaron Napotnik, my youngest brother, has been a beer connoisseur for years. He has travelled the world over multiple times, drinking craft beers everywhere he went. His experienced palate combined with August's brewing experience has been an excellent blend for great craft beer. Our relationship with craft beer as a family naturally led to us entertaining the idea of opening our own small craft brewery. We already owned the perfect building, so things just naturally fell into place.

How do you feel the internet has changed the way the craft brewing industry operates?

In the same ways that the internet has changed most industries, especially social media. People are more connected than ever to the businesses and brands they like to support. The internet, via social media, has infinite potential for tapping into a broad audience and promoting your brand at little to no expense. This allows us to really be a part of our community, which is important to us, and it seems to be important to the community.

What style of beer is your best seller and why do you think that is?

A Double IPA, dry hopped with citra hops. Because it is delicious.

Does glassware really make a difference?

Going back to "Atmosbeer," every little detail makes a difference. Skimping on details will be noticed. We try to be intentional about all the little details. Glassware is more than a small detail. We use a few different style glasses, which we serve with different beers, and it really does have an impact on the drinking experience. We don't use any crazy or odd shaped glasses, but they are solid quality and they feel great in your hand. Every little detail comes together to create an experience – for better or for worse.

What's the real difference between a Porter and a Stout?

Our head brewer, August Napotnik, says every brewer will probably have a different answer. Our simplified answer is not using roasted barley and keeping the ABV lower in the Porter – two characteristics that typically separate it from a Stout. A Stout is essentially, and historically, a more beefed up Porter.

EAGLEMONK PUB AND BREWERY

4906 W Mount Hope Hwy
Lansing, MI 48917

Dan Buonodono
Owner/Brewer

What year did you open and typically, how much beer do you guys make in a year?

We opened in 2012 and produce around 300 barrels a year

How much beer do you personally consume on an average workday?

2-3 pints

What's your favorite food to eat with beer and why?

Peanuts -- just goes well together

About how much does it cost to open a brewery?

Costs vary widely - Mine costed about $250k 8 years ago

In your opinion, if you were opening a brewery today what is the best BBL size to start with and why?

I do mostly "serve on premise, so 5BBL system would be better. I have a 7BBL system currently

When you first opened the brewery, what was the biggest obstacle? What advice would you give someone thinking about opening a brewery to avoid some pitfalls you experienced?

Biggest obstacle to me was dealing with state government

What separates breweries that don't make it in this business from the ones that do?

Business/Management skills - and brewing skills

How did you first discover craft beer and what made you want to enter the business?

Started homebrewing in 1982, and loved brewing beer ever since

What beer would you brew if cost, production, and sales were no object?

The ones I'm brewing now!

Do you think a new brewery should serve food or just beer?

I would not open a brewery without food on site

What beer is your brewery best known for and why?

Great beer and awesome staff!

End of a long brew day, what are you drinking?

Red Eye Rye!

ENID BREWING COMPANY

126 S Independence
Enid, OK 73701

Justin Blasier
Co-Owner & Brewmaster

Typically, how much beer do you guys produce in an average year?

We have been open for 1 year and I don't have the average just yet. We produced under 200 BBLs last year

How much beer do you personally consume on an average workday?

1 Pint

What's your favorite food to eat with beer and why?

Anything from our food menu. We pair the food with our beer. Personally I love our Cherokee Strip Chicken Tacos with our Vance Proud FlyPA (IPA)

About how much does it cost to open a brewery?

Add what you think.. then times that by 3. :-)

Do you think a new brewery should serve food or just beer?

We chose to start serving food.

In your opinion, if you were opening a brewery today what is the best BBL size to start with and why?

10-15 BBLS with a 1- 3 BBL Pilot System

What are today's worst beer trends?

Not caring about flavor or local grown grains.

What separates breweries that don't make it in this business from the ones that do?

Innovation.

In the past few years we have seen a massive surge in the popularity of Hazy IPA's and Sours, what do you believe the next popular beer style will be?

Local grown malt beers.

When you first opened the brewery, what was the biggest obstacle? What advice would you give someone thinking about opening a brewery to avoid some of the pitfalls you experienced?

Make is twice as big as you think you'll need. And start canning from day 1. Self distribute.

What beers are you best known for and why?

Our Pleasant Porter, Enterprise Amber Ale, and our Cielo Pintado (Painted Sky) Cerveza. All of our beer is made with local grown Oklahoma base malts. We are the first Grain to Glass brewery in the state.

What sets your brewery apart from most others?

We are the first Grain to Glass brewery in the state.

How do you decide on new beers to brew?

Test batches.

What are the biggest reasons for the continual growth of craft breweries?

People love local fresh beer. It brings people together and united people like nothing else!

What are the biggest obstacles to continued craft beer growth?

The bubble not bursting

What are the biggest problems you run into in producing beer?

Regulations

How do you reach beyond the hardcore beer drinkers and into the general public to sell your beer?

Make easier drinking beer.

How did you first discover craft beer and what made you want to enter the business?

Guinness expanded my taste. Boulevard Wheat made me brand out, Fat Tire made me love malt, a friend bought me a beer kit to make my own. That's the nutshell.

How do you attempt to increase beer production while still staying true to both your brand and your unique styles?

Increase capacity in innovative ways

What's the style most fun to brew?

Porter

What beer would you brew if cost, production, and sales were no object?

Porters, stouts, and ambers all the time.

Is there a popular beer you make that you just don't really like but everyone else loves?

American Light Lagers, Most from Big Beer Brands…flavorless carbonated water that try's to kill the little guys for no reason.

End of a long brew day, what are you drinking?

Cielo Pinatdo

What are a few beers that other brewers are making that you really find impressive?

Deez Nuts, by Nothings Left. It is a peanut butter porter.

How do you feel the internet has changed the way the craft brewing industry operates?

The internet has changed how every industry operates. In so many ways that this is a loaded questions. Ha!

When coming out with a new brew, how much experimentation do you do before you say it's ready for production?

At least one test batch.

What style of beer is your best seller and why do you think that is?

Cielo Pintado Mexican Cerveza. We have light beer drinking crowd that is just finding out about us.

Does glassware really make a difference?

Yes. It helps with brand recognition when you put it on your pints!

What's the real difference between a Porter and a Stout?

The name.

How important is IBU when it comes to picking out a beer? Do customers need to pay attention to it?

Only with eduction. But bitterness is very important.

ESTES PARK BREWERY

470 Prospect Village Dr
Estes Park, CO 80517

Typically, how much beer do you guys produce in an average year?

2500 bbls

How much beer do you personally consume on an average workday?

None I don't drink anymore I will taste it as needed.

What's your favorite food to eat with beer and why?

Beer really goes with any food. And from past experiences the more you drink the better the food tastes.

About how much does it cost to open a brewery?

Depends on what you put in but a full brewery with manufacturing at least a million with labor.

Do you think a new brewery should serve food or just beer?

We have a restaurant so I would say food the beer brings them in and the food makes the money.

In your opinion, if you were opening a brewery today what is the best BBL size to start with and why?

We have a 15bbl so I would say that otherwise you are brewing all the time.

What are today's worst beer trends?

I say it is hazy ipas it is just unfiltered.

What separates breweries that don't make it in this business from the ones that do?

Location and quality of beer.

In the past few years we have seen a massive surge in the popularity of Hazy IPA's and Sours, what do you believe the next popular beer style will be?

The good beers should always come back around and different trends depend a lot on the seasons.

When you first opened the brewery, what was the biggest obstacle? What advice would you give someone thinking about opening a brewery to avoid some of the pitfalls you experienced?

A lot of hard work and dedication and you can fail a lot at doing things.

What beers are you best known for and why?

Renegade IPA it won a gold metal at the great American beer fest in 1991, longs peak raspberry wheat, Stinger Wild Honey Wheat , Bear

Lake Blueberry Wheat and Red Rum Ale They are just all very clean beers.

What sets your brewery apart from most others?

Location, how long we have been around and quality.

How do you decide on new beers to brew?

Request for the consumer.

What are the biggest reasons for the continual growth of craft breweries?

People want a choice.

What are the biggest obstacles to continued craft beer growth?

Breweries could get a bad name if too many new ones start making bad beer and gives us a bad name.

What are the biggest problems you run into in producing beer?

Getting ingredients, time and demand.

How do you reach beyond the hardcore beer drinkers and into the general public to sell your beer?

Fests and advertising along with availability.

How did you first discover craft beer and what made you want to enter the business?

New Belgium in college just wanted to own my own business and why not beer.

How do you attempt to increase beer production while still staying true to both your brand and your unique styles?

Create a balance that works for your situation and times.

What's the style most fun to brew?

All ales.

What beer would you brew if cost, production, and sales were no object?

Barley wines and the wheats but they are already there.

Is there a popular beer you make that you just don't really like but everyone else loves?

No they are all good and fun.

End of a long brew day, what are you drinking?

Again just depends on the time of year i used to enjoy them all.

What are a few beers that other brewers are making that you really find impressive?

Bourbon stouts.

How do you feel the internet has changed the way the craft brewing industry operates?

Has not really affected me at all except everyone has an opinion even none beer drinkers. Does not always help us.

When coming out with a new brew, how much experimentation do you do before you say it's ready for production?

More research them experimentation been brewing for 25 years.

What style of beer is your best seller and why do you think that is?

The wheat beers everyone can drink them.

Does glassware really make a difference?

Not on beer it is more for looks I would say and how fast you can drink it.

What's the real difference between a Porter and a Stout?

Stouts are heavier and porters are smoother

How important is IBU when it comes to picking out a beer? Do customers need to pay attention to it?

Yes some people like high and some like low and a lot of times it depends on what they are doing or have to do (responsibilities)

EDGE CITY BREWERY

6209 Old Post Road - Ste 109
Charlotte, NC 28212

John Thomas
Operations Manager
Jared Thomas
Head Brewer

What year did you open and typically, how much beer do you guys make in a year?

We opened April of 2020. We are projecting to produce 500bbls our first year in operation.

How much beer do you personally consume on an average workday?

1-2 pints through sampling the beer in the unitanks.

What's your favorite food to eat with beer and why?

Beer cheese and pretzels or pizza.

About how much does it cost to open a brewery?

Our startup budget was 600k.

In your opinion, if you were opening a brewery today what is the best BBL size to start with and why?

We believe the best bbl size to start with would be a seven or ten barrel brewhouse system. In our opinion, this is the most economical system to start out on, you are able to produce enough beer for taproom and distribution. That being said, we opened on a 3bbl brewhouse system and we are making it work!

When you first opened the brewery, what was the biggest obstacle? What advice would you give someone thinking about opening a brewery to avoid some pitfalls you experienced?

Our biggest obstacle was navigating the environment surrounding Covid-19. We opened in the midst of the pandemic and were only able to sell to-go growlers. It is difficult to plan for everything that might go wrong but being able to pivot and adapt to changes quickly has been a big part of our success starting out.

What separates breweries that don't make it in this business from the ones that do?

We personally believe that there is not one thing that separates the success stories from the failures. We think having a well-rounded team, a clear understanding of your brand, vision and market, and definitely a passion for craft beer help towards becoming successful.

How did you first discover craft beer and what made you want to enter the business?

We grew up in Asheville, NC which has been voted "Beer City USA' a couple of time. Being able to be explore the craft beer scene in Asheville and finding our passion for brewing ultimately resulted in us opening up a brewery of our own.

What beer would you brew if cost, production, and sales were no object?

Lagers all day, everyday

Do you think a new brewery should serve food or just beer?

We think beer should be the main focus but food helps bring customers in and keeps them around longer.

What beer is your brewery best known for and why?

Having a variety of styles and flavors of beer for everyone to enjoy. Hazy's and sours are probably our most popular.

End of a long brew day, what are you drinking?

Probably a PBR.

EXPEDINTURE BREWERY

201 S 2nd Street
Okarche, OK 73762

Keith E. Griesel
Chief Operations Officer & Brew Meister

What year did you open and typically, how much beer do you guys make in a year?

We are a brand-new brewery. We opened 15 February 2020. Our projections for this year are around 500 bbl.

How much beer do you personally consume on an average workday?

If we are only talking about finished product, typically a pint or two. As brew master, I also taste product in various stages of fermentation throughout the day.

What's your favorite food to eat with beer and why?

My favorite food with beer would probably be any style of German sausage and kraut. Having spent time in Germany and being of German descent, sausage is just the food that I think of when I think of drinking good beer. A good German sausage can even make a mediocre beer tolerable.

About how much does it cost to open a brewery?

Cost to open a brewery depends on a lot of factors. When we were researching, we got answers that varied from well over $1 million to around $100,000. Those numbers all came from breweries in Oklahoma. It was not like that was the numbers we got from California and then the numbers from Oklahoma. We chose to buy land and build our own building, so it was more expensive up front for us. I would say having at access to at least $500,000 would probably be for the best.

In your opinion, if you were opening a brewery today what is the best BBL size to start with and why?

We started with a dual 5bbl brewhouse and have been extremely happy with it. I think having a plan for the type of brewery you want to be dictates size. If you are focused on taproom only session beers, a 5BBL is probably big enough but if your focus is distribution, you would need to go bigger.

When you first opened the brewery, what was the biggest obstacle? What advice would you give someone thinking about opening a brewery to avoid some pitfalls you experienced?

We found our biggest obstacle was second guessing ourselves. Every time we would decide on something, we would hesitate before execution trying to ensure we were doing the right thing. Once we got out of our own way, things went smoothly.

As for advice, expect the unexpected and just learn to roll with changes and hiccups. If you can figure out how to do that you should be good.

What separates breweries that don't make it in this business from the ones that do?

If you had asked that prior to COVID-19, I would have said quality of product. Now in a post COVID-19 world, I would say good financial practices and planning. Making great beer will always be the difference between keeping customers and not, but having access to funds in times of trouble will keep the doors open.

How did you first discover craft beer and what made you want to enter the business?

I first had really good beer when I was 16 and on a trip to Germany. When I was in college, I kept searching for those great German beers and that led me down a path that introduced me to craft beers. After a few more trips to Europe, I knew I wanted to try to brew those European style beers at home, so I got into homebrewing with a friend. People really loved our beers and I realized that I loved brewing for people. We decided to follow our passion and started working on a brewery after that.

What beer would you brew if cost, production, and sales were no object?

I was a historian and history teacher before becoming a brewer. If I could just brew things for me, I would brew historical beers. I don't think there are enough brewers doing that. Unfortunately, those beers typically have a limited audience and aren't great for the bottom line. Alternately, I also think if barriers were removed maybe a nice Oktoberfest would be my beer of choice.

Do you think a new brewery should serve food or just beer?

I think breweries must make that decision for themselves. We have a really great local restaurant across the street from us and two more within a couple of blocks. Therefore, food didn't make sense for us. People get food from the other places and bring it in to enjoy with our beer. It allows us to focus on what we are good at and not have to worry about food too.

What beer is your brewery best known for and why?

Our Irish Red Ale is probably our most popular beer and the one we are most know for. It is one of two beers we have up for distribution, and it is just a slightly sweet, smooth beer that people really seem to love.

End of a long brew day, what are you drinking?

Probably a lot of water, followed by our English Golden Ale or our Black Ale. The nice thing about owning a brewery, however, is that I don't have to pick just one thing. I can drink different beers on different days.

EAGLE PARK BREWING COMPANY

823 E Hamilton St
Milwaukee, WI 53202

Jake Schinker
Co-Owner, Idea Guy

What year did you open and typically, how much beer do you guys make in a year?

In our first year, 2017, we produced about 500 barrels. Three years later we are producing that same amount every month and still growing.

How much beer do you personally consume on an average workday?

Most of us have at least one beer a day after work before we go home. It's a great way to unwind a bit and regroup.

What's your favorite food to eat with beer and why?

Nothing beats a hazy IPA and some spicy curry.

About how much does it cost to open a brewery?

It's notoriously very expensive to start a brewery. Even though our growth has been rapid and our newest facility is our "dream brewery", we started off with very humble beginnings barely above the realm of homebrewers.

In your opinion, if you were opening a brewery today what is the best BBL size to start with and why?

A 10 barrel system is a perfect starting point to supply a busy taproom and also still have some left for distribution.

When you first opened the brewery, what was the biggest obstacle? What advice would you give someone thinking about opening a brewery to avoid some pitfalls you experienced?

Credibility...it takes a long time and lots of hard work to grow a following from scratch. You have to be patient yet diligent.

What separates breweries that don't make it in this business from the ones that do?

It's much easier to listen to what the people want than let your personal passions dictate the path of your brewery. Pride is good but sometimes it needs to be left at the door.

How did you first discover craft beer and what made you want to enter the business?

I started getting into beer later in college. I then got into homebrewing and met others who wanted to take the big step of turning a hobby into a career.

What beer would you brew if cost, production, and sales were no object?

Most days we brew anything we want but the key is balance. If you want to brew a mango habanero gose aged in tequila barrels, you should probably be three times as much pilsner and IPA.

Do you think a new brewery should serve food or just beer?

Never do anything you're not comfortable with. The restaurant industry is no walk in the park and adding it into your breweries business model can make or break the entire company in the blink of an eye.

What beer is your brewery best known for and why?

We are best known for our variety and constant innovation.

End of a long brew day, what are you drinking?

Something light and crisp, then if that went down fast I'll move to something more exciting.

ENERGY CITY BREWING

917 1st St
Batavia, IL 60510

Heidi Files
Co-Owner

What year did you open and typically, how much beer do you guys make in a year?

We opened in 2017 and we brewed about 1,500 bbls in 2019.

How much beer do you personally consume on an average workday?

We like to sample our own creations and the new beers released by our fellow breweries. It probably averages out to a beer or two per day.

What's your favorite food to eat with beer and why?

Mostly we enjoy sampling the beers on their own to get the full flavor profile. Some of our fruity beers pair great with spicy foods. Our hazy beers go well with more traditional meals like pizza.

About how much does it cost to open a brewery?

There is such a range in breweries that you can probably start a nanobrewery with as little as $50,000 and the sky is the limit on how expensive it can go up to.

In your opinion, if you were opening a brewery today what is the best BBL size to start with and why?

Smaller breweries have more flexibility and carry less debt. We'd recommend a smaller size for starters. We started ours with a one barrel system. Contract brewing and alternating proprietorships offer the flexibility to try different brewery sizes until you find the right fit.

When you first opened the brewery, what was the biggest obstacle? What advice would you give someone thinking about opening a brewery to avoid some pitfalls you experienced?

We would suggest to listen to your customers, start small and master the art of brewing before putting in lots of capital into a taproom. Reach out to people or organizations that have assistance for small businesses. We had great assistance from our Chamber of Commerce, our local SBA office, our Mainstreet organization and even the City staff and elected officials. The more you communicate with others, the more you will find those who want to help your brewery to succeed. Also, get a good accountant!

What separates breweries that don't make it in this business from the ones that do?

Offer a great experience for your customers. Whether that's in your tap room or with the packaged product people enjoy on their own time. Maintaining customer relations is very important. Being able to adapt is critically important in the craft beer industry right now.

How did you first discover craft beer and what made you want to enter the business?

Our brewmaster is a chemical engineer and was given a start-up brewing kit that his wife bought at a garage sale 15 years ago. It got him interested in the brewing process and developed into an extensive hobby and eventually a business.

What beer would you brew if cost, production, and sales were no object?

If money wasn't an object and label approvals and designs and marketing and time for pilot batches weren't an issue, we would probably brew a new beer every week! For small craft breweries, variety seems more important compared to brewing a specific beer all the time. Even the very best craft beer right now won't be trending in a year or two.

Do you think a new brewery should serve food or just beer?

We prefer to focus solely on beer. Food trucks are a great option for small startup breweries. Adding food is like adding a whole new business to your brewery!

What beer is your brewery best known for and why?

Ask us in a year and our answer will be different. Our Brewery is known for pioneering new beer types and making beer that is sought after. Just look for us at the forefront of the trending styles.

End of a long brew day, what are you drinking?

David the brewmaster would be drinking water since he likes to head out for a jog after a long day stuck in the brew house. Heidi, his wife and co-owner likes to sample the beers or savor a low ball of high-end tequila.

FIELDS & IVY BREWERY

706 E 23rd St
Lawrence, KS 66046

Cory Johnston
Founder\CEO

Typically, how much beer do you guys produce in an average year?

We have been brewing 11 months. We are on track for 1,000 bbls our first year.

How much beer do you personally consume on an average workday?

If I'm working, less than 16oz

What's your favorite food to eat with beer and why?

Anything that is well made and a thoughtful pairing. We do pizza, burgers and wings at our brewpub those are all really good with beer. If drinking stronger flavored beers I prefer to drink them without food or with something bland as a palate cleanser.

About how much does it cost to open a brewery?

There's a brewery for every budget.

Do you think a new brewery should serve food or just beer?

Depends on the market and the owner's budget. If you're in a strong craft beer market where you can attract beer drinkers without offering food and you really want to focus on beer then that would be ideal. Many markets will require breweries to also offer food in order to bring people in the door people who may drink wine or cocktails but be willing to come in with their buddy that likes beer. IMO food, wine, cocktails improves number of customers and improves the energy level of the establishment and that makes the beer experience better.

In your opinion, if you were opening a brewery today what is the best BBL size to start with and why?

There is not a best size. It depends on the local market. I started with a 20 bbl system because that's how much beer I felt I needed to sell to be able to hire top brewing talent.

What are today's worst beer trends?

Lactose.

What separates breweries that don't make it in this business from the ones that do?

Something like 95% of breweries have been making it. That's amazing but will probably change during the Coronavirus pandemic. As a brewery owner I feel like any weak spot could potentially be a cause of failure.

The first 11 months of being open have been a constant mad scramble for cashflow, improving products, improving service, improving customer satisfaction. There are 1,000s of breweries competing for the same beer dollar that you are. Instant and constant feedback on social media if your product isn't meeting expectations.

In the past few years we have seen a massive surge in the popularity of Hazy IPA's and Sours, what do you believe the next popular beer style will be?

Pilsner. Ha ha. We keep saying that and it never happens. The next popular style will probably have IPA in the name. The next popular style will have fruit in it. The next popular style will appeal to a wider set of beer drinkers.

When you first opened the brewery, what was the biggest obstacle? What advice would you give someone thinking about opening a brewery to avoid some of the pitfalls you experienced?

Money. Don't quit your day job. Do not expect to execute Plan A. Be flexible and optimistic. Everything will take twice as long as cost twice as much as you expected. Pinch every penny. Hire good consultants if you don't know what you are doing. They will pay for themselves many times over. If you can't afford good consultants and you don't know what you're doing than you need to find a partner that has real professional experience – not someone that read a book.

If you decide to open a restaurant you need an experienced partner. Period. Work out some kind of contract. Your experienced partner should have at least 10 years of experience RUNNING a PROFITABLE restaurant. And, hire a competent lawyer to draw up a real contract.

Locate your brewery in a location appropriate for your business model. People will not "find you" if you are in a shitty location.

What sets your brewery apart from most others?

We are able to brew with locally grown grains. Like idiots we built a pretty big brewery and packaging line right off the bat. It's very stressful and hard to make money but we have kick ass talent in the brewery and those folks make great beers.

How do you decide on new beers to brew?

Look at the market, what sells, what do we want to drink that we can't find? What can we make with local ingredients? What historical or new styles inspire our curiosity? I personally like to develop beers that challenge our brewers. I like to take a historical style and add something modern or local. Beer that tastes good.

What are the biggest reasons for the continual growth of craft breweries?

Beer culture is mostly a social thing and craft breweries give people in an area something to experience and talk about.

What are the biggest obstacles to continued craft beer growth?

Unfair competition, taxes.

What are the biggest problems you run into in producing beer?

Making money

How do you reach beyond the hardcore beer drinkers and into the general public to sell your beer?

Make beer the general public cares about.

How did you first discover craft beer and what made you want to enter the business?

Red Hook ESB on a trip to San Francisco a million years ago. I always liked beer but the packaging and beer were so unique that it finally clicked to me that beer could be a local, cool thing that had unique flavor versus big beer. Maybe it was the first ale that I liked? It was cool and different.

How do you attempt to increase beer production while still staying true to both your brand and your unique styles?

Not a problem at our scale.

What's the style most fun to brew?

I'm the owner, not a brewer, so I don't know.

What beer would you brew if cost, production, and sales were no object?

Mixed ferm, wood aged stuff with tons of fruit and cool stuff in it.

Is there a popular beer you make that you just don't really like but everyone else loves?

No

End of a long brew day, what are you drinking?

Whatever I need to drink for QA, typically. I still love drinking with my friends and co-workers, doing a bottle share, trying new stuff.

What are a few beers that other brewers are making that you really find impressive?

I need to know how it's made to be impressed. Anything with layers of interesting flavor that's balanced enough to be a pleasure to drink.

How do you feel the internet has changed the way the craft brewing industry operates?

Yes.

When coming out with a new brew, how much experimentation do you do before you say it's ready for production?

We talk about it a lot. We do bench testing when we can. We taste commercial examples when we can. We drain pour if it's not right.

What style of beer is your best seller and why do you think that is?

IPA. It costs the most to brew and has pretty low margin typically. People instinctively know value.

Does glassware really make a difference?

Yes. It's part of the experience. But, when you have beer in distribution it better taste good out of a plastic pint glass because that's how it's going to be served eventually. We did a tasting event at an account that served our 10.5% bourbon barrel aged stout in a 22oz frosted mug (for $6). It was freaking awesome and we all had one and got a great buzz.

The best thing about running a brewery is the customers. People that come in, draft accounts, off-premise accounts, festival goers. Those are the beer lovers and the interactions that make us feel good about what we do.

What's the real difference between a Porter and a Stout?

Roasted barley

How important is IBU when it comes to picking out a beer? Do customers need to pay attention to it?

It's pretty important. If we had all the time in the world we would like to offer beer education courses at our facility and at other liquor stores or draft accounts. Educating staff and drinkers about flavor characteristics helps them choose beers that they will enjoy.

FRIENDSHIP BREWING COMPANY

100 Pitman Ave
Wentzville, MO 63385

Brian

Typically, how much beer do you guys produce in an average year?

At present about 1500 barrels, but we just purchased a larger second location.

How much beer do you personally consume on an average workday?

One or two, sometimes zero.

About how much does it cost to open a brewery?

At bare minimum a half million and that is light.>

Do you think a new brewery should serve food or just beer?

Food for sure.

In your opinion, if you were opening a brewery today what is the best BBL size to start with and why?

At least 15bbl. Economy of scale and labor costs coupled with growth capability.

What are today's worst beer trends?

The milkshake mess, glitter for sure (I think it died thankfully), and I'm tired of NEIPA's already.

What separates breweries that don't make it in this business from the ones that do?

Business knowledge and practices. A lot of very talented brewers have little or no business sense.

In the past few years we have seen a massive surge in the popularity of Hazy IPA's and Sours, what do you believe the next popular beer style will be?

Hopefully clean, well executed classic styles. Lagers, pilsners, classic english/german/Belgian brews.

When you first opened the brewery, what was the biggest obstacle? What advice would you give someone thinking about opening a brewery to avoid some of the pitfalls you experienced?

Be very wary of partners/investors! Be very financially stable, have contingency money on hand.

What sets your brewery apart from most others?

A very cool historic taproom, enormous patio/beer garden, clean beers and friendly people.

How do you decide on new beers to brew?

Listen to patrons, and give our head brewer the ability to experiment.

What are the biggest reasons for the continual growth of craft breweries?

A decline in interest and support of large corporate beers, people love local. They want to have a personal connection to the brewery.

What are the biggest obstacles to continued craft beer growth?

Big Beer continuing to make daily attempts to crush craft.

What are the biggest problems you run into in producing beer?

Staffing in the retail setting, costs of goods sold in the marketplace.

How do you reach beyond the hardcore beer drinkers and into the general public to sell your beer?

Give them approachable beers, connect with them via events and fundraisers.

How did you first discover craft beer and what made you want to enter the business?

Drinking quality beer on a study abroad program in London 30 years ago.

How do you attempt to increase beer production while still staying true to both your brand and your unique styles?

Increase volume of sales with the same passion and dedication, no scrimping.

What's the style most fun to brew?

Belgians

What beer would you brew if cost, production, and sales were no object?

Rum and bourbon aged stouts and big Belgians (and barleywines).

Is there a popular beer you make that you just don't really like but everyone else loves?

Our biggest seller! Its a blonde and boring but sells like crazy!

End of a long brew day, what are you drinking?

Session IPA

What are a few beers that other brewers are making that you really find impressive?

Nothing beats what the abbey boys brew!

How do you feel the internet has changed the way the craft brewing industry operates?

It has allowed for hyper trendy beers to be revered via manufactured scarcity.

When coming out with a new brew, how much experimentation do you do before you say it's ready for production?

Small batch release.

What style of beer is your best seller and why do you think that is?

Lagers, approachable!

Does glassware really make a difference?

To a degree yes, but it's impractical in a busy taproom.

What's the real difference between a Porter and a Stout?

A porter is a session stout.

How important is IBU when it comes to picking out a beer? Do customers need to pay attention to it?

Semi important, only true hopheads pay attention, and they know that an IPA doesn't have to have a big IBU number to be tasty.

FOR THE LOVE OF GOD BREWING

2617 W Northwest Blvd
Spokane, WA 99205

Steve Moss
owner/operator/and brewer

Typically, how much beer do you guys produce in an average year?

We produce around 140 bbl per year.

How much beer do you personally consume on an average workday?

I might have 1-2 beers on an average work day.

What's your favorite food to eat with beer and why?

I am a big foodie so if its really good food, than I say pair it with really good beer.

About how much does it cost to open a brewery?

I can only speak to our experience on this one. I worked construction for the past 18 years. So we saved a lot on our tap room buildout. We spent around $75,000 to get our place up and running with a 2 bbl brew house.

Do you think a new brewery should serve food or just beer?

I am a big fan of food with beer, so I like to see at least a small plate menu at a brewery.

In your opinion, if you were opening a brewery today what is the best BBL size to start with and why?

I believe in this market the best approach is small and nimble. I do wish we could have started slightly bigger than we did though. I would say 5-7 bbl brewhouse would be a great place to start.

What are today's worst beer trends?

I'm not to psyched on the carbonated alcohol water that some breweries are producing. Its simple sugar, fermented with flavoring, and in my opinion it's no good for the industry, or for the consumer.

What separates breweries that don't make it in this business from the ones that do?

I believe quality will always be the main equation between failure and success. But having a cool tap room, and friendly personable staff goes a long ways as well.

In the past few years we have seen a massive surge in the popularity of Hazy IPA's and Sours, what do you believe the next popular beer style will be?

I'm not sure exactly, but I think the pendulum always searches for balance. Some of the more popular beers today are a bit on the sweet side,

I wouldn't be surprised to see the balanced out by some dryer more drinkable beers.

When you first opened the brewery, what was the biggest obstacle? What advice would you give someone thinking about opening a brewery to avoid some of the pitfalls you experienced?

We didn't see any huge pit falls in opening. Money is always a concern though. We didn't have investors, so we came up with all the money ourselves. Just remember that its true you will likely spend double, or even triple what you had originally budgeted for. Also TTB licensing was very slow, get your TTB app in ASAP!

What beers are you best known for and why?

We have made a name for ourselves with pastry sours, and low IBU IPA. We also make pastry stouts, some pilsners, and even a Gruit here and there. But we have found that our sours are the main beer that people come back for.

What sets your brewery apart from most others?

We are doing some pretty unique beers at least in our area. I think that is the biggest factor in our standing out among the crowd. We also took great care in building a space that is both unique, and inviting.

How do you decide on new beers to brew?

I pretty much brew whatever beer I want, and hope that people love it. I try to have a well thought out recipe that ties with our brand. Other than that, I just try to keep sours on tap at all times.

What are the biggest reasons for the continual growth of craft breweries?

I'm not certain why craft breweries have had such incredible growth over the last several years. I do think that the consumer is more informed these days and that with that information they are making decisions based and quality, rather than price AKA choosing craft over macro breweries. There is also some very exciting stuff happening in the brewing scene these days, Milkshake IPA, fruited sours, pastry stouts.

What are the biggest obstacles to continued craft beer growth?

All I can say is that There are a lot of breweries right now and I'm not sure how sustainable this growth is. Hopefully we will see more beer drinkers due to the more accessible styles, and more current drinkers switch from macro to craft.

What are the biggest problems you run into in producing beer?

There are a lot of off flavors that can occur in a finished beer. Those are a continual battle to keep out of your beer. We are very strict about dumping beer that is less than we deem worthy. On a small scale brewery like ourselves, you don't have some of the advantages that other larger breweries have to maintain perfect yeast pitches, and perfect temperatures at all times. We definitely do our absolute best to up hold quality, but it can be a struggle.

How do you reach beyond the hardcore beer drinkers and into the general public to sell your beer?

We strive to produce beer that pretty much anyone will enjoy. Your not gonna win them all though, so just remember to stay true to your passion. People are smart, and they can tell if something is genuine.

How did you first discover craft beer and what made you want to enter the business?

I discovered craft beer pretty early on. I drank some domestic lagers, and immediately started searching out more flavorful beers. I became so passionate about craft beer that I started brewing my own. It was pretty much a spiral effect after that.

How do you attempt to increase beer production while still staying true to both your brand and your unique styles?

Our goal is just slow organic growth. Keep quality as the number 1 priority, and stop to think and pray about any big decisions.

What's the style most fun to brew?

I really enjoy brewing sours. We are working on getting our coolship setup so we can start brewing spontaneous beer and that is extremely exciting to me.

What beer would you brew if cost, production, and sales were no object?

Definitely spontaneous, and mixed Ferm sours.

Is there a popular beer you make that you just don't really like but everyone else loves?

I don't really produce a beer that I don't like. If I didn't like it, then it would probably go down the drain before the consumer had a go at it. I have made a fruit loop IPA that was popular, but definitely not my top choice.

End of a long brew day, what are you drinking?

Either a sour, a IPA, or pilsner.

What are a few beers that other brewers are making that you really find impressive?

Burial brewing produces some stouts that are mind blowing! Also tree houses IPA make me completely green with envy.

How do you feel the internet has changed the way the craft brewing industry operates?

Obviously there is way more advertising via social media now. It also makes sharing beer ideas pretty easy. But then it kinda makes every brewery in the world your competition rather than just the ones in your back yard.

When coming out with a new brew, how much experimentation do you do before you say it's ready for production?

We live in the realm of experimentation here at FTLOG. With a 2 bbl system you can kinda just go nuts, and we have. We've made Oreo beers, fruit loop beers, spruce tip beers, mint and blueberry beers, and all kinds of crazy adjuncts and fruit.

What style of beer is your best seller and why do you think that is?

Sours, sours, sours. We make some unique, fruity, sours that people just seem to go bonkers for. We maintain a lower acidity level in our sour beers which may be why so many people seem to enjoy them.

Does glassware really make a difference?

Yes it does. In particular it makes a difference for the aroma and head retention.

What's the real difference between a Porter and a Stout?

I was hoping you could tell me!? I have actually never brewed a porter. Porters tend to taste more ashy, roasty, vs chocolatey like stouts.

How important is IBU when it comes to picking out a beer? Do customers need to pay attention to it?

IBU is dead for the most part. It's not an accurate gauge for true perceived bitterness in todays beers. We need a new bitterness scale ASAP.

FOULMOUTHED BREWING

15 Ocean St
South Portland, ME 04106

Craig Dilger

What year did you open and typically, how much beer do you guys make in a year?

June of 2016, currently making about 1,000 BBL a year.

How much beer do you personally consume on an average workday?

None of your god damn business!

What's your favorite food to eat with beer and why?

Local beef burger, medium rare.

About how much does it cost to open a brewery?

Anywhere from about $100K to $20M depending on scale

In your opinion, if you were opening a brewery today what is the best BBL size to start with and why?

I wouldn't start less than 5BBL. 10 or 15BBL systems provide the best expansion options.

When you first opened the brewery, what was the biggest obstacle? What advice would you give someone thinking about opening a brewery to avoid some pitfalls you experienced?

Managing the set up and it's inherent expense. However much you have budgeted for the brewhouse and tanks, just plan to spend at least that much on installing it all unless you are a certified electrician, plumber, mechanical/hvac engineer.

What separates breweries that don't make it in this business from the ones that do?

Sadly I think it is mostly about having adequate capital to start up and a solid business plan to back it up. You need to know that you'll be able to sell enough beer to pay your bills before you even start building. That means already knowing your distribution strategy and having a real sense of what quantities you or distributor will be able move and what those margins will look like and being certain that will cover your bills.

How did you first discover craft beer and what made you want to enter the business?

I discovered craft beer at The Old Toad in Rochester, NY while studying at RIT. I have always been a curious sort who like to try to make things for myself, so I progressed through being a home brewer to being a professional cellar person, assistant brewer, etc while slowly assessing the industry and writing a business plan.

What beer would you brew if cost, production, and sales were no object?

Exactly what we are making now. One specific style over and over is boring, brewing a broad selection of new and old styles alike is what keeps the craft fun.

Do you think a new brewery should serve food or just beer?

I think the paring of food and beer is an important one and we take great pride in having exceptional food to pair with our beers. But running a restaurant is a lot of work so partnering with nearby restaurants and food trucks could save a lot of headache and expense if the area allows it.

What beer is your brewery best known for and why?

Probably our Yuzu Koshō Gose, a citrusy and slightly spicy sour ale that uses a traditional Japanese condiment (Yuzu Koshō) for it's salinity and unique flavor.

End of a long brew day, what are you drinking?

Probably something of the German persuasion. A Helles or a Schwarzbier depending on the weather and my mood.

FOUR STACKS BREWING

5469 N US Highway 41
Apollo Beach, FL 33572

Nathan Hangen
Owner/Operator

What year did you open and typically, how much beer do you guys make in a year?

We opened in October of 2015, and we make about 300-500 bbl/year

How much beer do you personally consume on an average workday?

Most of the brewers/owners sample product all day every day (in very small quantities), so we don't have much of an appetite for drinking after work. We may have a pint or two a few times/week, then indulge a bit more on the weekends with product we've brought home.

What's your favorite food to eat with beer and why?

My favorite food with beer is pizza because it's simple and easy to eat. I am not a fan of beer or food snobs, and my appetite reflects that.

About how much does it cost to open a brewery?

It really depends on the size, if you are leasing/buying, etc. I would say that you need a minimum investment of 200-250k plus 50k/month savings for the first 3-6 months of service.

In your opinion, if you were opening a brewery today what is the best BBL size to start with and why?

We started with 1.5 BBL and then upgraded to 3 BBL. We would like to upgrade to 5-7 BBL, but it's about twice the cost. I think 3 BBL is a great size because you can then convert the system into a test system once you upgrade.

When you first opened the brewery, what was the biggest obstacle? What advice would you give someone thinking about opening a brewery to avoid some pitfalls you experienced?

The biggest obstacle was all of the legal and administrative challenges you face to get started, approved to open, and approved to stay open. It's a non-stop battle of paperwork, hiring/firing, managing schedules, ordering, etc.

What separates breweries that don't make it in this business from the ones that do?

Being under-capitalized. You will never have enough money.

How did you first discover craft beer and what made you want to enter the business?

I discovered it through my many travels to San Diego and visiting Stone Brewing, Ballast Point, Green Flash, etc. I wanted to build something as impressive here as they had done there.

What beer would you brew if cost, production, and sales were no object?

I would brew 20 different kinds of lagers/pilsners and really have fun with treatments, classical styles, and light beers in order to make craft beer more approachable, and combat the macro-breweries as they encroached on our turf. I love many different styles, but it's easy to get burned out on the fancy stuff, and I've had enough of it to last a lifetime. I'm all about clean and simple flavor profiles these days.

Do you think a new brewery should serve food or just beer?

I recommend serving snacks of some sort, and food trucks can be flaky, so planning a kitchen is probably a smart idea if you have the budget.

What beer is your brewery best known for and why?

We're known for our DIPA, Octopus Prime. People love the name, but also love the high ABV, heavy hop profile, and complex malt backbone. It pays homage to the West Coast style IPAs we love.

End of a long brew day, what are you drinking?

Our Lou Dog blonde ale, or our Interloper IPA. Both light and easy to drink.

FORT SMITH BREWING COMPANY

7500 Fort Chaffee Blvd
Fort Smith, AR 72916

Quentin Willard
Owner/Brewer

Typically, how much beer do you guys produce in an average year?

300 BBL

How much beer do you personally consume on an average workday?

2 pints

What's your favorite food to eat with beer and why?

Bread and meat, they seem to compliment beer well. Also, they are the easiest to get your hands on and it's busy around the brewery so convenient food is usually the go-to.

About how much does it cost to open a brewery?

$500,000 on the low end

Do you think a new brewery should serve food or just beer?

I think that depends on the market. If there are plenty of food establishments around then the brewery could get away with not serving food. I'm also a purist and believe everyone should stay in their lanes. Do you want a brewer making your beer and food or just your beer? Do you want a chef making your beer and food or just your food? Let the professionals do what they do best and not overstretch themselves. Now pairing a great brewmaster with a great chef would make for the perfect environment.

In your opinion, if you were opening a brewery today what is the best BBL size to start with and why?

5-7BBL. Any smaller and you'll be spending most of your time brewing and less time working on the business. A bigger system will allow you to manage demand and spend adequate time on training staff and other aspects of a successful start-up.

What are today's worst beer trends?

Seltzer

What separates breweries that don't make it in this business from the ones that do?

So many variables. One main issue I've seen is partnership disputes.

In the past few years we have seen a massive surge in the popularity of Hazy IPA's and Sours, what do you believe the next popular beer style will be?

Fruity. Fruity anything

When you first opened the brewery, what was the biggest obstacle? What advice would you give someone thinking about opening a brewery to avoid some of the pitfalls you experienced?

Local politics. Have a good lawyer or be very influential in the community you're opening up in OR just move to a community that is brewery friendly.

What beers are you best known for and why?

Stout and Saison because they are traditionally liked by a large group of people but ours are palatable for many many taste buds.

What sets your brewery apart from most others?

We opened in a very business unfriendly community and have slowly been converting them to supporting small business.

How do you decide on new beers to brew?

Usually the customers come up with them.

What are the biggest reasons for the continual growth of craft breweries?

It's a great product, number 1. But number 2, breweries are more than beer. They are the bedrock for communities everywhere!

What are the biggest obstacles to continued craft beer growth?

Marketing from the big guys. Also, the big guys buying craft breweries and putting sheep skin over them as if they are craft beer. The big breweries craft beer portfolio is like a wolf in sheepskin. Eventually they'll slowly start closing them all down and then it'll be like American beer in the 70s again.

What are the biggest problems you run into in producing beer?

Keeping up with demand.

How do you reach beyond the hardcore beer drinkers and into the general public to sell your beer?

Providing other services at the brewery besides beer. We do a lot of cross promotions with other businesses to get people in the doors and once they get past the initial perception that all craft beers are hoppy the beer sells itself.

How did you first discover craft beer and what made you want to enter the business?

In New England and it was the craft beer community that appealed to me. The industry is like no other industry in that they help each other succeed.

How do you attempt to increase beer production while still staying true to both your brand and your unique styles?

The million $ question

What's the style most fun to brew?

IPA

What beer would you brew if cost, production, and sales were no object?

Quadruples and Double IPAs

Is there a popular beer you make that you just don't really like but everyone else loves?

IPAs. I like them too but they are a pain to brew.

End of a long brew day, what are you drinking?

Depends on if it was a successful brew day or not.

What are a few beers that other brewers are making that you really find impressive?

Quads

How do you feel the internet has changed the way the craft brewing industry operates?

We have a chance to beat out the marketing money of the big guys because of the internet.

When coming out with a new brew, how much experimentation do you do before you say it's ready for production?

Not as much anymore.

What style of beer is your best seller and why do you think that is?

Saison, it's fruity enough and light enough and beer enough to appeal to every tastebud.

Does glassware really make a difference?

For sure

What's the real difference between a Porter and a Stout?

Strength of the roasted malts

How important is IBU when it comes to picking out a beer? Do customers need to pay attention to it?

Depends on what the customer wants.

FACTOTUM BREWHOUSE

3845 Lipan St
Denver, CO 80211

Laura
(co-owner)
Chris
(co-owner and head brewer)

What year did you open and typically, how much beer do you guys make in a year?

Feb 2015, 200 BLLs

How much beer do you personally consume on an average workday?

2-3 beers - Laura (and Chris)

What's your favorite food to eat with beer and why?

Cheese with malty beers and spicy food with tart beers. The perfect complement! - Laura

Spicy asian noodle dish, because a beer helps wash away the heat - Chris

About how much does it cost to open a brewery?

In 2014/2015 before the marijuana boom in Denver, you could bootstrap a decent brewery for $500K

In your opinion, if you were opening a brewery today what is the best BBL size to start with and why?

Depends on your goal. Taproom only? 4 BBL. Want to distribute? probably at least 10BBL

When you first opened the brewery, what was the biggest obstacle? What advice would you give someone thinking about opening a brewery to avoid some pitfalls you experienced?

Lack of information and organization within the city government. It's still an ongoing problem. They wasted a LOT of our time while rent money was just flying out the door. Advice? Talk to breweries that are already open in your municipality (or even just restaurants/bars) and find out what hassles they had. If we had known we would've opened up 5 miles away and outside of city limits

What separates breweries that don't make it in this business from the ones that do?

Poor money management (3 mortgages on your house!?! What!?), poor people management. How much money you have as reserves. Secondarily, probably the ability to create hype about your product whether it's warranted or not.

How did you first discover craft beer and what made you want to enter the business?

College in the late 90s at CU Boulder. My brother is our head brewer, this was his dream. I jumped on his bandwagon :) - Laura

College at the Gunnison, CO brewery (my first IPA!). It was a natural evolution from hobby to passion to career - Chris

What beer would you brew if cost, production, and sales were no object?

Fresh fruited beers; saisons, pale ales, sours... - Laura

Argentinian IPA (can't get the hops here in CO) - Chris

Do you think a new brewery should serve food or just beer?

Doesn't matter to me. Managing food costs/inventory on top of running a taproom seems like a nightmare.

What beer is your brewery best known for and why?

Imperial Kentucky Common or our Glorieta Colorado IPA - both are solid, well -made beers that are just different enough that you can't find anything similar within the vicinity.

End of a long brew day, what are you drinking?

Coors Banquet :) - Laura (co-owner)

Upslope Lager - Chris (co-owner and head brewer)

THE GLASS JUG BEER LAB

5410 NC-55 suite v,
Durham, NC 27713

Chris Creech
Co-Owner / Brewing Operations

Typically, how much beer do you guys make in a year?

We are currently brewing about 300-350 bbls/year

How much beer do you personally consume on an average workday?

I don't consume much on workdays. I may take a couple small QA samples on any given day in the brewery and then have a pint after work or with dinner.

What's your favorite food to eat with beer and why?

It really depends on what I'm in the mood for and what beer I'm pairing it with. A crisp, refreshing Mexican-style lager with tacos from a local taco truck is hard to beat. But, I'll also take an IPA with a cheeseburger on a Friday night.

About how much does it cost to open a brewery?

This is a vague and somewhat ridiculous question. It depends on so many different factors. It could be anywhere from as low as $200k up to many many millions based on the size of the brewery, renting/buying the building, how much upfit is needed, taproom size, etc., etc.

What are today's worst beer trends?

I'm not a fan of the over-sweetening of beer. We're seeing it with all of the adjunct-heavy "pastry" stouts, as well as with the hazy IPAs. There is a lot of residual sugar left in these beers which, to me, make them harder to drink. I prefer crisp, dry beers. But, I still don't think the trend is bad, necessarily, as it has opened up craft beer to new segments of the population who otherwise probably wouldn't have tried/liked less-sweet beers.

When you first opened the brewery, what was the biggest obstacle? What advice would you give someone thinking about opening a brewery to avoid some pitfalls you experienced?

This could be a whole book and I don't have the time for all of this. But, the biggest obstacles were funding, keeping construction anywhere near budget, and the design/layout of the physical brewery space. My advice would be to talk to people who have done it before, but not just out of the blue. If you're opening a brewery, you better already have established good friendships/relationships with other brewers. Buy them a few beers to go over some of this stuff with you.

How do you decide on new beers to brew?

Customer demand, styles that fit within our brand, and a desire to keep a wide range of options available on tap

How did you first discover craft beer and what made you want to enter the business?

I discovered craft beer in college by way of beers like North Coast Red Seal Ale, Sierra Nevada Pale Ale, and Sam Adams Boston Lager. I got into homebrewing shortly thereafter and through my friendships and connections within that community, became interested in entering the industry. We first opened a retail beer and wine shop with a small bar and only about 3 years later added an on-site brewery.

What beer would you brew if cost, production, and sales were no object?

I'd continue to brew a variety of styles, but I'd have less hesitation about trying some of the less "sexy" styles like dark lagers or an English mild.

Does glassware really make a difference?

Yes

What beer is your brewery best known for and why?

We're known for small experimental one-off batches that are mostly only found in our taproom. We're branded as a "beer lab," so our experimental nature is at the forefront. We're also widely recognized because we are both a brewery and a retail craft beer and wine shop all under one roof, which people really enjoy.

End of a long brew day, what are you drinking?

Pilsner.

Which hop varieties do you find yourself using most often and why?

Citra and Mosaic because they are the most heavily used in our IPAs and crowd favorites. We also like to try out lots of new varieties, but these two are always finding their way into our IPA recipes.

What was the first beer you ever brewed and how did it taste?

As a homebrewer in college, the first beer I made was a brown ale and I thought it was delicious. I didn't know a whole lot at the time, so I'm certain it had some faults, but right then, it was an amazing beer.

GRINDHAUS BREW LAB

Hercules Space Center Industrial Park,
1650 N Hercules Ave Unit I,
Clearwater, FL 33765

Lisa Colburn

What year did you open and typically, how much beer do you guys make in a year?

About 100 BBL.

How much beer do you personally consume on an average workday?

Not much, maybe a pint. When I'm at work it's all business.

What's your favorite food to eat with beer and why?

Depends on what beer pairs well with the food. Beer is much like wine with food pairing.

About how much does it cost to open a brewery?

Depends upon the brewery size. Around 100k for a small nanobrewery.

In your opinion, if you were opening a brewery today what is the best BBL size to start with and why?

It really depends upon the location. Right now the model for success is a nanobrewery without distribution. Start small, 1-3 BBL and add from there.

When you first opened the brewery, what was the biggest obstacle? What advice would you give someone thinking about opening a brewery to avoid some pitfalls you experienced?

The biggest obstacle was all the licensing requirements. Talk to other brewery owners for questions, consider consulting an attorney that specializes in helping breweries.

What separates breweries that don't make it in this business from the ones that do?

With breweries it seems like the big issue for failure is being undercapitalized and having too much debt. Make sure to have plenty of operating capital and keep the overhead low.

How did you first discover craft beer and what made you want to enter the business?

I started drinking craft beer in 1991 and homebrewing in 1995. A friend talked me into opening my first brewery in 2012.

What beer would you brew if cost, production, and sales were no object?

Fortunately we're small and have many beers on tap, so I can Brew whatever I want.

Do you think a new brewery should serve food or just beer?

I think if they don't have a kitchen there needs to be food options close by.

What beer is your brewery best known for and why?

Probably our Jalapeno-Tomatillo Berliner Weiss because it's so unique.

End of a long brew day, what are you drinking?

Usually our smoked red ale, it has complexity but goes down easy. I'm just looking for something to relax with at that point.

GATLINBURG BREWING COMPANY

1349 E Parkway
Gatlinburg, TN 37738

Steve C. Wilson

Typically, how much beer do you guys produce in an average year?

We are currently producing 250 bbls annually. Almost complete is our new location where we hope to produce 3000 bbls annually.

How much beer do you personally consume on an average workday?

Currently I don't drink on workdays. When I did though, I'd say 2-3 pints at the end of a shift. With it so readily available you have to watch your consumption. I don't keep the lbs off like I used to lol.

What's your favorite food to eat with beer and why?

Pizza! We make the best pizza!

About how much does it cost to open a brewery?

I've witnessed breweries open for $20,000 and in to the millions. I guess it comes down to where your ambition and your means intersect.

Do you think a new brewery should serve food or just beer?

I think a new brewery should serve whatever their market allows. It's expensive to open and sustain a brewery. If selling food, liquor, wine, merchandise ect. helps you pay your rent I'm all for it.

In your opinion, if you were opening a brewery today what is the best BBL size to start with and why?

Speaking from a personal viewpoint, I like smaller to start. (5-7 bbls) It keeps the cost low while getting familiar with your market. If the demand is there you'll have time to build the big one later.

What are today's worst beer trends?

I'll refrain from bashing any trend. Seems like these days everyone tries to ride the next new wave.

What separates breweries that don't make it in this business from the ones that do?

Lack of capital/cash flow is probably the biggest. I also think there are a lot of great brewers that may not be great businessmen or vice versa. Successful breweries have to have both.

In the past few years we have seen a massive surge in the popularity of Hazy IPA's and Sours, what do you believe the next popular beer style will be?

Craft Lagers

When you first opened the brewery, what was the biggest obstacle? What advice would you give someone thinking about opening a brewery to avoid some of the pitfalls you experienced?

Finding inexpensive but sufficient equipment. Until the business can buy new buy used. I almost feel like you need to earn new equipment lol. Struggle first appreciate later lol. Also, handle the ttb yourself. An attorney is expensive and a little reading and self confidence will save a lot.

What beers are you best known for and why?

Breakfast Juice NEIPA and Don't Feed the Bears (DFTB) an English Brown Ale. I like to think its because they are excellent beers. While this may be the case I think it says more about our customers. The majority of our customers are new to craft beer and both beers are very inoffensive.

What sets your brewery apart from most others?

Our staff!!! Family is not cliche round here!

How do you decide on new beers to brew?

Collectively! We all sling ideas until one sticks. For us, these days it's more about keeping up with the core brands than experimenting.

What are the biggest reasons for the continual growth of craft breweries?

Personally I think it's just the cool thing right now. The culture is contagious, quality is great, and it's fresh.

What are the biggest obstacles to continued craft beer growth?

Competition! As the numbers increase more people are fighting for the same piece of pie. It will eventually become more about business and less about craft.

What are the biggest problems you run into in producing beer?

Our personal nemesis is hop availability.

How do you reach beyond the hardcore beer drinkers and into the general public to sell your beer?

We like to make what we call "crawl before you walk beers." By that we mean an inoffensive craft beer. High in quality but not a single overbearing flavor. Craft beer with training wheels if you will. We want to make a beer for everyone and sometimes that means compromise.

How did you first discover craft beer and what made you want to enter the business?

I go into depth on our website but this is the short version. I went to an Outkast concert. They had 2 beers for sell. Pabst Blue Ribbon and Sierra Nevada Torpedo. They were both 16oz cans and only a difference of $1 while significantly different in alcohol content. The choice was made for me and am I glad it was. The aroma of hops had me hooked and I've been a changed man since.

How do you attempt to increase beer production while still staying true to both your brand and your unique styles?

We stay consistent with our processes. 5 gal or 500 it all comes down to 3 p's People, Percentages, and Processes!

What's the style most fun to brew?

Personally I enjoy brewing west coast ipa's. They make the whole place smell amazing.

What beer would you brew if cost, production, and sales were no object?

Sours! we have yet to dip our toes in that water yet.

Is there a popular beer you make that you just don't really like but everyone else loves?

"Gatty Light" While I love the name, cost to produce, and sales volume its just not my style of beer. You realize that's like picking your least favorite kid right??

End of a long brew day, what are you drinking?

G.P.A. Gatlinburg Pale Ale a session west coast style IPA

What are a few beers that other brewers are making that you really find impressive?

Elst Brewing "Gruit Ale" Last days of Autumn "Parden My Garden IPA" Ecusta Brewing "First Descent IPA"

How do you feel the internet has changed the way the craft brewing industry operates?

I feel like it makes everyone an expert even if their favorite beer is the color of water and in a blue can.

When coming out with a new brew, how much experimentation do you do before you say it's ready for production?

It's ready when it's ready!

What style of beer is your best seller and why do you think that is?

NEIPA it's the hot topic right now.

Does glassware really make a difference?

It only makes a difference if the person using it says so.

What's the real difference between a Porter and a Stout?

These days just the name

How important is IBU when it comes to picking out a beer? Do customers need to pay attention to it?

IBU's only tell part of the story. If your looking for the beer with the most IBU's your probably also looking for the 72oz steak to eat in less than an hour lol.

GIG HARBOR BREWING CO.

3120 South Tacoma Way
Tacoma, WA 98409

John Fosberg

What year did you open and typically, how much beer do you guys make in a year?

Gig Harbor Brewing Co. opened just after Thanksgiving 2015. The response was very positive, even with two other local micro breweries opening the same month.

We started with a 10bbl brewing system and three 10bbl fermentors. Over the past four and a half years, we've added four 20bbl fermentors, a new large cooler, a canning machine, etc. Typically we produce upwards of 1,500 bbls per year — and we're still not at full capacity.

How much beer do you personally consume on an average workday?

I drink from a 10 oz. glass so I can sample a wide variety of our beers four-five days a week — anywhere from 20-40 oz. per day. This routine allows me to taste our full line up of flagship, seasonal, and one-off brews. And it is a great way to keep our taproom staff on their toes and in touch with our taproom patrons. We have a very loyal customer base — and a strong Mug Club at both taproom locations — and people seeing and mingling with the owner makes a big difference in connecting to your customers on a personal level. We get a tremendous amount of very valuable feedback and great ideas from listening to our customers in the taprooms.

What's your favorite food to eat with beer and why?

1. Hotdogs/Brats

2. Why: Ballpark.

3. Enough said.

About how much does it cost to open a brewery?

A lot more than I thought...ha ha! Since recruiting our first investor 3 years before we opened, over $750,000 has been spent on our initial build-out, three brewery expansions, a second taproom location, etc. If I was doing it again today, I would create the pro forma budget and then simply double everything.

In your opinion, if you were opening a brewery today what is the best BBL size to start with and why?

I would never do anything under 10bbl, which was our minimum size when we started. Volume is so important. Every taproom customer, grocery store, bar, and restaurant has their favorite Gig Harbor Brewing beer and if you run short, they're unhappy (pissed). And then you run the risk of losing a customer, shelf space, a tap handle, and losing even one is unacceptable.

If I was doing again, I would not consider anything smaller than a 20bbl brewing system.

When you first opened the brewery, what was the biggest obstacle? What advice would you give someone thinking about opening a brewery to avoid some pitfalls you experienced?

In the very beginning, direct sales to local bars and restaurants was our biggest obstacle. We didn't have an experienced professional beer seller, and we were too new for local distributors to care yet. So when we first started, our taproom was initially our strongest form of revenue.

Since opening in 2015, we have partnered with two local distributors for several years, broken ties with those two same distributors, and gone back to a self-distribution model, but with a seasoned beer sales professional. This mix seems to work best for us, but everyone is different.

Another obstacle was we worked so hard on the build out in the brewery, and making sure that the beers we produced for our opening were of highest quality, that I think we fell short on having all our marketing cogs in order. Our business plan, branding, and graphic design were strong, but our execution of PR, guerilla marking opportunities, social media, and working with local business organizations, etc. wasn't completely in place when we first opened.

What separates breweries that don't make it in this business from the ones that do?

Great consistent beer; great simple marketing; and the best people you can possibly find.

In the early years, while shopping the Gig Harbor Brewing business plan around, I was given some great advice from an owner that was about to open his new brewery: "Hire a professional brewer, not a home-brewer trying to take it to the next level, or your buddy from college, but a seasoned professional that already knows how to brew on a large system. No matter how long they've been doing it, or how confident they are in their skills, home brewers and professional brewers are not the same."

Having that conversation with a new brewery owner inspired me to spend the money on a professional brewer with over 15 years of commercial brewing experience. Doing so, made all the difference in having our beer recipes already dialed in when we first opened our doors, and as we introduce new beers every year.

Sometimes it really pays to listen.

How did you first discover craft beer and what made you want to enter the business?

My other marketing company started producing the Gig Harbor Beer Festival back in 2011. That's where I met a lot of brewers, did a lot of research, and started conceiving the plan for Gig Harbor Brewing. During that time I was looking for something new to do in my life, and all the brewers seemed to be having such a good time, I decided I'd found what I was looking for.

What beer would you brew if cost, production, and sales were no object?

Rows and rows of whiskey-barrel-aged beer stacked to the ceiling. And we have some pretty high ceilings.

Do you think a new brewery should serve food or just beer?

Great question. Everyone is different, but, as a production brewery, food seems a distraction to me. Here in WA State there are different levels of food permits that will allow you to do different things with food offerings. So, if your model — and your dream — is to be a brew pub, go for it.

I have talked to many taproom visitors who think we're nuts not to have a kitchen, but these folks usually have never owned, run, or worked in a restaurant, and have no concept of the amount of labor, costs, and regulations required. And the tiny profit margins.

I believe as long our taproom customers know they can bring in whatever they want, order in from local restaurants that deliver, and use apps for food delivery services for just about any restaurant around, why not avoid the extra food costs, staff costs, cleaning costs, health department inspections, etc. (a.k.a. headaches).

Focus on the beer.

What beer is your brewery best known for and why?

Giggly Blonde. I mean, look at that can design! Plus, it is delicious and great for any season or occasion. And an excellent way for non-craft beer drinkers to take that first step.

Ghost Ship Imperial Stout is an award-winner for us as well. This brew started as a seasonal, but turned out to be so popular and versatile (we've barrel-aged it, made a black cherry stout with it, casked it, and put it on nitro gas, etc.) that we now brew it year around.

End of a long brew day, what are you drinking?

Sturdy Gertie Dbl IPA…mmmmmmm…I'm having one now.

GARRETT'S MILL & BREWING COMPANY

8148 Main St
Garrettsville, OH 44231

Nick Greco

What year did you open and typically, how much beer do you guys make in a year?

2018 and 96 barrels

How much beer do you personally consume on an average workday?

16-32 oz

What's your favorite food to eat with beer and why?

Smoked food such as chicken wings or thighs or pork.

About how much does it cost to open a brewery?

$100,000-$750,000

In your opinion, if you were opening a brewery today what is the best BBL size to start with and why?

A 4 barrel brewhouse is a middle sized (volume) system allowing a brewery to produce 850 pints per batch ensuring a steady supply to the taproom on a reasonable brewing schedule (2-3 times per week). This sized system allows brewer flexibility and creativity between batches for a reasonable sunk cost per batch (consumable cost of $150-$400) depending on the style.

When you first opened the brewery, what was the biggest obstacle? What advice would you give someone thinking about opening a brewery to avoid some pitfalls you experienced?

Establishing client-desired and accepted brews consistent with current style expectations. Review current style trends, review client demographics and routine styles enjoyed by clients, and review styles previously brewed by the brewer. Listen to customer comments and educate a diverse customer base who are highly likely to be light lager consumers and not ale normally produced by small breweries.

What separates breweries that don't make it in this business from the ones that do?

Brew products accepted by consumers and for brewer flexibility.

How did you first discover craft beer and what made you want to enter the business?

In the 1990 enjoying Ballantine IPA and Miller's Reserve series especially their porter. There was the budding appreciation of ale versus the popular lagers which dominated the industry.

What beer would you brew if cost, production, and sales were no object?

The "new" style of New England IPA. A smooth, restrained bitter ale with significant percentages of flaked oats and wheat.

Do you think a new brewery should serve food or just beer?

Both. Especially, if the food selections compliment the beer. This emphasizes a creative relationship between the cuisine and brewhouse enhancing the consumer experience.

What beer is your brewery best known for and why?

The Ma Barker is an industry-unique birch/rootbeer ale brewed with local maple syrup, a retrained bitterness, pure vanilla, and lactose for slight residual sweetness.

End of a long brew day, what are you drinking?

A low IBU New England IPA or Scottish ale preferably with the latter whiskey barrel aged.

GLOUCESTER BREWING COMPANY

6778 Main St
Gloucester, VA 23061

Myron Ware

What year did you open and typically, how much beer do you guys make in a year?

Opened Dec 2018 with a 7bbl system, producing 300bbl our first year in 2019, and on track to repeat or go slightly higher in 2020.

How much beer do you personally consume on an average workday?

Just the shift-pint all our employees are entitled to.

What's your favorite food to eat with beer and why?

Love pizza, or pulled pork - the flavors seem to naturally go together

About how much does it cost to open a brewery?

That's almost too open-ended. If you buy a building, then much more than if you rent a space. We got a favorable lease, but paid for all the buildout of the space to turn it from a shell of a building into something that could house a brewery. And then the cost of the equipment itself to brew/keg/store beer for sale. For us, $400k would be a close approximation, but there are too many variables to consider: size and condition of building, size of brewhouse, are you distributing (keg counts), are you doing any of the work yourself, etc.

In your opinion, if you were opening a brewery today what is the best BBL size to start with and why?

If distributing, 10bbl, with at least one 20bbl FV and BT so that you can double batch some recipes as needed for demand. Work up a calculation to see how much beer you'll need to sell and at what cost/pint to cover your expenses, how much room you'll have in your cooler at any given time for new kegs of beer, and work backwards to find out how much beer you'll need to make in a year.

When you first opened the brewery, what was the biggest obstacle? What advice would you give someone thinking about opening a brewery to avoid some pitfalls you experienced?

Biggest obstacle was getting our 1930's-era building capable of brewing beer - there was a lot more buildout needed than we'd anticipated. And the equipment was over a month late being delivered, so that set our timetable back to a winter opening from a fall opening. If you have friends that are engineers, architects, contractors, etc, use those connections to reduce the up front costs of design and buildout. Use your county's grant system to secure funding, and use crowdfunding to give an influx of cash to keep your buildout projects funded. We were successful with that aspect, and built a large deck on the side of our building with those funds, exceeding our goal by 15-20%.

What separates breweries that don't make it in this business from the ones that do?

I think you need to have a firm grip on what your market is looking for in a beer. Our market would be classified as not-so-out-there, so we're not trying to produce a sour-of-the-month, or avant-garde lemon-pepper-nutmeg-candy-stripe concoctions - just solid beer that our patrons enjoy. You've got to realize what the popular mass-market beers are that the market is likely consuming, and give them choices that will introduce them to the joys of the craft experience.

How did you first discover craft beer and what made you want to enter the business?

I've been homebrewing since 1991. A local article highlighted that a study done suggested that Main street would greatly benefit from a microbrewery and it started there.

What beer would you brew if cost, production, and sales were no object?

They're all relatively similar in cost, but I'm partial to IPA and stouts

Do you think a new brewery should serve food or just beer?

Just beer. Food service requires a whole other set of permits and will potentially be a big drain on the bottom line. Employ local food trucks instead.

What beer is your brewery best known for and why?

We have to make our IPA once a month now, and our cream ale is a hit with those that have a palate more in line with the mass market light beers.

End of a long brew day, what are you drinking?

I had an IPA yesterday

GROSSEN BART BREWERY

1025 Delaware Ave Unit A
Longmont, CO 80501

Taylor Wise

What year did you open and typically, how much beer do you guys make in a year?

2014 around 600bbls

How much beer do you personally consume on an average workday?

3

What's your favorite food to eat with beer and why?

Nothing particular

About how much does it cost to open a brewery?

10bbl size about 200 to 500k

In your opinion, if you were opening a brewery today what is the best BBL size to start with and why?

10bbl easy to go to 20bbl brews

When you first opened the brewery, what was the biggest obstacle?

Finding money

What advice would you give someone thinking about opening a brewery to avoid some pitfalls you experienced?

Wouldn't do it today too saturated

What separates breweries that don't make it in this business from the ones that do?

Product quality

How did you first discover craft beer and what made you want to enter the business?

Sierrra Nevada Pale Ale, to make beer better!

What beer would you brew if cost, production, and sales were no object?

Pilsner

Do you think a new brewery should serve food or just beer?

It definitely helps

What beer is your brewery best known for and why?

Our Chin Curtain IPA an Stubble Kolsch, Number one sellers

End of a long brew day, what are you drinking?

One of our Handle Barley Wine Series, Barley Wines

GOOD WORD BREWING & PUBLIC HOUSE

3085 Main St Ste 520
Duluth, GA 30096

Todd DiMatteo
Owner/Brewer

What year did you open and typically, how much beer do you guys make in a year?

Good Word opened Nov. 28th 2017, and we make around 800bbls a year. We are a brewpub with a full kitchen and bar.

How much beer do you personally consume on an average workday?

I try and not drink on the week/workdays. It's at challenging at times for sure.

What's your favorite food to eat with beer and why?

There are some really good Szechuan food near us and our Die Todd Die Pilsner is great with their spicy food.

About how much does it cost to open a brewery?

It varies greatly. Depending on what size brewhouse and cellar, your rent or mortgage, and what all packaging equipment you decide to purchase along with it. You could open a brewery for $25-30k or spend $3-5million or much much more.

In your opinion, if you were opening a brewery today what is the best BBL size to start with and why?

We have a 10bbl kit and that's a great size in my opinion. Get as many fermentors as you can, and at least one or two brites and try and get a decent canning line, a small one if you are limited with budget. Like the Wild Goose Gosling. Being able to put beer in cans from day one will make things easier in my opinion.

When you first opened the brewery, what was the biggest obstacle? What advice would you give someone thinking about opening a brewery to avoid some pitfalls you experienced?

Make sure you find a really good contractor for your buildout. And also make sure YOU pay the sub contractors directly. This is a huge piece. Also find a place that really wants you. The city of Duluth (Georgie) where we are has been one of our greatest allies.

What separates breweries that don't make it in this business from the ones that do?

A great product is where you start. Also strong branding and messaging can not be overlooked. Make sure your social media presence is strong and start building your audience as soon as you have a building locked in. I am an owner here, our only brewer, and our social media person. I'm busy but if I can make it work and have success you can too.

How did you first discover craft beer and what made you want to enter the business?

I've been around craft beer for over 15years now. I worked at Brick Store Pub in Decatur and it's easily one of the best beer bars and has been for almost 25years. I love to cook and brewing was a natural extension of that. Once I started I was hooked. I love it.

What beer would you brew if cost, production, and sales were no object?

We would order some horizontal 20bbl fvs, at least 2, but 4 would be perfect, and up our lager production. I usually have 2-3 on draft (prepandemic) and they are some of my favorites to make and drink.

Do you think a new brewery should serve food or just beer?

I think a new brewery should be driven by the creatives that had the passion to start the dream in the first place, serving food was a given for us because my partner and i had a lot of restaurant experience, but you should do whatever feels right.

What beer is your brewery best known for and why?

Never Sleep ipa. It's a 7% double dry-hopped ipa with Vic Secret, and citra. It's juicy, has a balanced bitterness, and a soft full mouthfeel.

End of a long brew day, what are you drinking?

Our Italian Pilsner we brewed in collaboration with Blackberry Farm. It's called "Any Day Now" 5% dry-hopped with Mittlfruh directly shipped from Seitz Farm in Germany. Make Good beer, but don't worship it.

HELIX BREWING CO.

8101 Commercial St
La Mesa, CA 91942

Cameron Ball

What year did you open and typically, how much beer do you guys make in a year?

Opened: August 2015. Production:~500 bbls/year

How much beer do you personally consume on an average workday?

1-2 pints

What's your favorite food to eat with beer and why?

Pizza, it goes with every style of beer and smells great when it is being made and you're enjoying that first pint :)

About how much does it cost to open a brewery?

Depends on the production size/model, but super off the cough numbers are around $1M.

In your opinion, if you were opening a brewery today what is the best BBL size to start with and why?

10-15 bbls and do on site tasting room for the majority of beer sales. It keeps the beer fresh, distribution and packaging costs to a minimum and allows the brewery to play with unique hops to make the customer happy with new beer styles when they visit.

When you first opened the brewery, what was the biggest obstacle? What advice would you give someone thinking about opening a brewery to avoid some pitfalls you experienced?

The biggest obstacle is sticking to a budget. As the project advances, new ideas constantly come to mind which comes with a cost. One must stay focused on the original plan and only implement if funds are available or can be moved from another aspect of the project (while still benefiting the complete project).

What separates breweries that don't make it in this business from the ones that do?

Delicious beer and comfortable atmosphere to drink it in.

How did you first discover craft beer and what made you want to enter the business?

I was an avid homebrewer in college.

What beer would you brew if cost, production, and sales were no object?

Session IPA and Pilsner

Do you think a new brewery should serve food or just beer?

A new brewery should serve whatever they are passionate about. If they love making food then share their food creations with everyone else. If they just love making beer, then leave the food to a food truck who has a passion for cooking.

What beer is your brewery best known for and why?

Tasty IPAs, family-friendly staff and a comfortable atmosphere. People describe Helix as drinking beer in their best friends backyard.

End of a long brew day, what are you drinking?

Session IPA, or whatever beer another brewer dropped off :)

HILLSBOROUGH VINEYARDS & BREWERY

36716 Charles Town Pike
Hillsboro VA 20132

Tolga Baki
Owner and Head Brewer

What year did you open and typically, how much beer do you guys make in a year?

Belly Love Brewing opened in 2014 with a capacity of ~500bbl, Hillsborough Farm Brewery was added to Hillsborough Vineyards in October of 2018 with a capacity of 1,100bbl which can be doubled if needed.

How much beer do you personally consume on an average workday?

Thats a funny misconception that we sit around and drink all day. I sample beers from tanks, and might have a beer after work, but I prefer bourbon in my glass typically.

What's your favorite food to eat with beer and why?

Neither a favorite food or a favorite beer. Depends on my mood, the setting, and the company. I usually like nibbles with beer since I usually drink it socially

About how much does it cost to open a brewery?

Sky is the limit. Depends if you want to be a brewpub, small nano, or a package brewery. Also depends greatly on location, and rent. I would say from $200k to millions

In your opinion, if you were opening a brewery today what is the best BBL size to start with and why?

Not a chance in hell I would open one today.

When you first opened the brewery, what was the biggest obstacle? What advice would you give someone thinking about opening a brewery to avoid some pitfalls you experienced?

I had businesses before, so for me production planning was the biggest challenge. Keeping a steady supply chain, always having hops and ingredients available, etc...

What separates breweries that don't make it in this business from the ones that do?

Business sense and knowhow. Too many hobbyists and homebreweres that treat it like their personal bar. Some make good beer, some don't. Few know how to run a business.

How did you first discover craft beer and what made you want to enter the business?

College… Apparently there were these concoctions that didn't come in a 24 pack of cans for $12. I didn't have much money, so I went for the most volume. I recall my first was Sam Adams Boston Ale… not sure they make that anymore. First sip was disgusting. I mean… what was all this "flavor" beer was supposed to be like water so you can shot gun it. Second sip was eye opening. Third sip and I think I pissed myself. Started buying all the craft I could which was clearly VERY limited in the late 80's. Bought a TON of imports and really enjoyed the Belgians the best.

What beer would you brew if cost, production, and sales were no object?

They aren't on a small scale. I brew what I want… except sours which thankfully I don't really like anyway.

Do you think a new brewery should serve food or just beer?

Food is necessary. Again, it's a social thing.

What beer is your brewery best known for and why?

Belly Love is known for Flying Unicorn Crotch Kick. A very expensive double IPA made with mosaic and galaxy. Also another unique beer called Duke, which is a Belgian Triple with starflower making the beer change colors from steel blue to bright purple depending not the ambient light. Hillsborough is known for it's dry hopped Pilsner, Hillsbräu, and it's Belgian Blonde, Blonde Moment.

End of a long brew day, what are you drinking?

Bourbon.

HORSE & DRAGON BREWING COMPANY

124 Racquette Dr
Fort Collins, CO 80524

Carol Cochran

What year did you open and typically, how much beer do you guys make in a year?

We opened in May of 2014. In 2019 we made 2830 barrels of beer (so we are still one of the small tykes). In 2020 we are crossing our fingers to hit 900 barrels, despite the most promising first quarter we've ever had to a year. That all came to a screeching halt in March/April due to COVID-19, and we don't anticipate a return to our previous barrelage for several years, unfortunately.

How much beer do you personally consume on an average workday?

Virtually none during the workday (we do taste fermenting beer and finished beer — so maybe a few ounces a week), but 3-4 pints a day after work, either visiting accounts or with dinner.

What's your favorite food to eat with beer and why?

We have a quote up in our brewery uttered by our friend Vijay Parmar: "Good food, without beer, is pointless." We wholeheartedly agree. There's not a food that exists that isn't better when paired with the right beer. The layers of flavor and the carbonation that cleanses your palate readying it for the next bite — exquisite. The most flexible beers we brew for food are our Picnic Rock Pale Ale and Whistle Blast Honey Brown. They each go with a pretty large variety of dishes. But every single style of beer can be paired with one dish or another to make a 1+1=3 experience. We love that part of the craft industry!

About how much does it cost to open a brewery?

It depends on a million factors — your location (and the real estate costs there), proximity to ingredients, size of system and number of fermenters you plan to invest in, whether or not you need to buy cooperage for distribution or you are using some other solution for getting your beer to consumers (e.g., serving tanks in a tasting-room-only model), how many people you're going to need to help run your operation, etc. Unless you're thinking of a nano-sized operation, the biggest initial expense is the stainless (brewhouse and fermenters); those figures are relatively easy to estimate and depend on your anticipated size and your chosen supplier's costs. [Our only advice here is be sure to invest enough to get a system that's not going to detract from your beer during production — sometimes things are on sale or inexpensive for a reason, and your product quality depends largely on how your system is going to treat your beer.] Then of course the biggest ongoing expense is people. Factor all that in and you've got your "how much does it cost." It's not a way to get rich, for most of us, despite a few mind-boggling buyouts everyone's read about. But it's sometimes a way to break even, support several other people, be an integral part of your community, and work in an industry and with a product you love.

In your opinion, if you were opening a brewery today what is the best BBL size to start with and why?

Again, this depends on your location, how many other breweries are selling to your anticipated market, and how much beer you need to sell to support your people (and yourself, hopefully!). There's recently been a huge trend among consumers for hyper-localization, so opening a small neighborhood brewery would seem to be the way to go. But 10 years ago everyone's goal seemed to be regionalization. And that changed in a matter of 2 years. So it's pretty hard to predict what would be the most sound approach for what the market will look like 10 years from now. Of course, the smaller you are, the more you're going to depend on direct to retail sales, because you just don't have access to the economies of scale needed to give up any margin on wholesale sales to bars/restaurants/distributors. So your model will help determine the size of system you need.

When you first opened the brewery, what was the biggest obstacle? What advice would you give someone thinking about opening a brewery to avoid some pitfalls you experienced?

The biggest surprise to us was the cost of stainless welding and the hard piping setup. But if the next craft brewery owner factors that in to her/his business plan accurately, there'll be some other line item they miss on by a long shot. Building some flexibility (financial and emotional) into your business plan is key, so that a few of those shocks don't overwhelm you.

What separates breweries that don't make it in this business from the ones that do?

I can't tell you. I would say, go in clear-eyed so that you're not disillusioned when you realize it takes a ton of hard work to support your people and yourself (even more than you thought when you thought you were being clear-eyed), and it takes years of that hard work. And love your product and your community. I think those three things will shave your odds for success. After that, I don't know that there's a magic key. We know breweries we think make great beer that have gone under and ones we think make mediocre beer that thrive.

How did you first discover craft beer and what made you want to enter the business?

A million years ago, as a senior in college, my then-boyfriend, now husband and business partner, took me to the first craft brewery that opened near where we went to school. The beer was so much more delicious than anything we'd been drinking that we were immediate converts and have spent the intervening 35 years exploring craft anywhere we live or travel.

What beer would you brew if cost, production, and sales were no object?

I feel guilty admitting this, but flavor-wise we've brewed everything we have wanted to brew (and continue to do so). We've brewed almost about 200 recipes since we opened, and continue to branch out from that. But we would very much like to use a higher percentage of grains from our local craft maltsters (we have 2 local partners who are making amazing malts) to better support them. We use some of their grains in all of our beers and a couple of times a year we make an all-local brew, but it would/will be pretty great to go 100% local craft malt in our recipes when we can afford it.

Do you think a new brewery should serve food or just beer?

Serving food adds many layers of complexity but also encourages patrons to stay for another round and treat your location as a gathering place. I'm preaching against what we're trying to build here at Horse & Dragon, because we committed to being a partner to bars and restaurants and we operate "just" a small tasting room at the brewery (trying not to compete with our local bar and restaurant customers). The margins on this, as I mentioned previously, are lower, and at our smaller size, it's hard to make this model work. It requires a lot of people power to support those retail partners. But we like the interconnectedness of this model within the communities to which we sell.

What beer is your brewery best known for and why?

Sad Panda Coffee Stout, which is a relatively light-drinking, year-'round stout (somewhere on the continuum between stout and porter — but we labeled it a stout and it stuck). It's a great base beer with chocolate malts, a good roast reminiscent of coffee to begin with, and then additions of chocolate, cold-pressed organic coffee, and vanilla. None of those flavors overwhelm it, though — the goal in every case where we make such additions is to make a really great base beer that is nuanced with the additional flavors. We're not sure why that's the beer people know from us — a combo of the name, and the fact that there must have been a hole in the market for a lighter stout. We strive to make every single beer a great and tasty representation of its style, so it's not the only beer we brew that we think is delicious. But for some reason, it hit some folks' spot. (Luckily for us!)

End of a long brew day, what are you drinking?

A pale ale — usually our Picnic Rock Pale Ale. I love the hops on pales that are largely unobstructed by their malt bills. IPAs often have such complex malt bills that the hops don't shine through as much as they do with American pales.

HERBIERY BREWING

Madison, Wisconsin

Nick Ryan
Founder & Brewmaster

Writers Note: Herbiery is a brewery which contracts the production of beer, made with sustainably sourced herbs and spices in place of hops, through another local craft brewery in Madison, WI.

What year did you open and typically, how much beer do you guys make in a year?

I started the company in January of 2018 and our production began in July of 2019. This first year we'll make about 120 bbls and will hopefully ramp up to 500 to 1,000 bbls in the next couple years.

How much beer do you personally consume on an average workday?

Not much, maybe half a beer as a weekly average. If I'm going to buy beer, I want it to be something unique or something with a flavor I'm excited about at the time. I'm not one for stocking my fridge with a steady supply of macro cans. Buying local and supporting a locally circular economy feels important to me.

What's your favorite food to eat with beer and why?

Hard cheeses melt the strength of stronger flavored beers like imperials or intensely bitter beers like a mugwort or dandelion pale ale. Red meat goes great with some of the sage or fennel beers I make. I think about food when I create recipes a lot, people tend to drink and eat at the same time so this feels like an important thing to consider. Since I'm totally unconstrained by hops, I can create beers with herbs and spices that complement just about any food.

About how much does it cost to open a brewery?

I've been working off of a $100,000 credit line for 2.5 years which I've only used about 3/4 of in those 2.5 years. Contracting production and self-distribution saves me a lot of money on the front end here. I can only speak from personal experience and most people do not start breweries from a contract production direction.

When you first opened the brewery, what was the biggest obstacle? What advice would you give someone thinking about opening a brewery to avoid some pitfalls you experienced?

I would have encountered more obstacles if I hadn't asked for so much help. No one knows every in and out of starting one of these things and there are experts just chomping at the bit to help people looking to bring more craft beer to the market. Find a small business consultant, ideally through local university programs if you live near a university as those are often free. Create financial projections for your first five years and make sure the consultant or a financial advisor is helping you with those numbers. Reach out to regulatory agencies at both the federal and state level, often your permit application or organization will be assigned an agent and becoming friends with this person can make hurtling through the regulatory hoops a lot easier.

What separates breweries that don't make it in this business from the ones that do?

Having the time and resources to do thorough market research on your intended brand aspects like beer styles, taproom aesthetic, social media, mission and vision. If you can thoroughly flesh out the mission and vision, and thus answer why you're starting a brewery, you can lean on that belief system when things get hard. Financial planning and projection for your first five years which you work on every couple months to update or make sure you're staying on track. Also, when I was able, I empowered CPAs, attorneys, consultants, and fellow brewing industry folks to both give me advice and work for me; paying these people when appropriate is worth it.

How did you first discover craft beer and what made you want to enter the business?

I discovered craft beer through my studies of herbalism. I wanted to make beer using herbs and spices like people used to do before the hop takeover in the 14th and 15th centuries but with modern improvements and updated recipes. Before then I had a fairly casual relationship with craft beer. When I had been homebrewing for a couple years I knew I had something unique to bring to the market. By then I was deep in craft beer and had thoroughly explored what the current market had to offer. My discovery that the market didn't offer many herbal or spiced beer and no hop free beer was what really set me on my mission to corner this niche market.

What beer would you brew if cost, production, and sales were no object?

I would collaborate with local farmers from each bio-region of the united states to create a beer with locally grown herbs/fruit/spices on top of the same malt base that could then be distributed solely in the region it was produced.

What beer is your brewery best known for and why?

I've only been producing commercially for 10 months but we make a Sage Wit with sage, coriander, and grapefruit peel that was popular and polarizing. People are also big fans of the Zingibeer ginger lager.

End of a long brew day, what are you drinking?

A michelada with homemade bloody mary mix and a crisp local pilsner.

HELLBENT BREWING

13035 Lake City Way NE
Seattle, WA 98125

Randy Embernate
Owner/ Head of Sales and Marketing

Typically, how much beer do you guys produce in an average year?

It's been growing every year. But 2800 bbls a year is the average.

How much beer do you personally consume on an average workday?

I consume about 6 beers a week. But not one everyday. I usually drink a few twice a week.

What's your favorite food to eat with beer and why?

I like meat and cheese plates preferably, but anything salty works for me. Another fav is a hot dog! It makes the beer taste better, and in turn makes the food taste better.

About how much does it cost to open a brewery?

For a decent size brewery, i would say $500,000 to $1,000,000. That would set you up pretty well.

Do you think a new brewery should serve food or just beer?

I think serving just beer works, but there needs to be food available (at the location) hopefully there is enough food trucks to come to, and WANT to come to you establishment. Food keeps them there, and in return, probably means more beer sales.

In your opinion, if you were opening a brewery today what is the best BBL size to start with and why?

15 bbl system is a good start. With room for more fermentation tanks.

What are today's worst beer trends?

Worst beer trends....hmm I don't really think any beer trend are the worse. To me, it is what it is.

What separates breweries that don't make it in this business from the ones that do?

I think a strong taproom is what keeps you in business. Ones with great location and a great set up will do well.

In the past few years we have seen a massive surge in the popularity of Hazy IPA's and Sours, what do you believe the next popular beer style will be?

Next trend... Lagers

When you first opened the brewery, what was the biggest obstacle? What advice would you give someone thinking about opening a brewery to avoid some of the pitfalls you experienced?

Biggest obstacle... conflict in ideas. Getting on the same page with your team. Lots of different ideas of what should happen.

What beers are you best known for and why?

IPA, done well!

What sets your brewery apart from most others?

We have a great taproom in a great neighborhood.

How do you decide on new beers to brew?

Everyone gives their ideas and suggestions to the head brewer, and he pretty much just decides when and what we brew.

What are the biggest reasons for the continual growth of craft breweries?

Lots of new beers and a great customer base keeps craft beer growing. Everyone wants the newest beer/brewery

What are the biggest obstacles to continued craft beer growth?

Lots of competition

What are the biggest problems you run into in producing beer?

Keeping up with demand, and not moving certain skus fast enough

How do you reach beyond the hardcore beer drinkers and into the general public to sell your beer?

We make our taproom approachable, a public gathering space. And if they want a beer, they will at least try our beer, or a flight. Then they will hopefully find something they like

How did you first discover craft beer and what made you want to enter the business?

I bartended for 18 years, served a lot of beer. Worked at a sports bar with lots of taps, lots of craft beers. Got into knowing what I sell. I always wanted to own a bar, and why not a brewery. Worked out better because I was brought in for my sales, wholesale is something that I like doing.

How do you attempt to increase beer production while still staying true to both your brand and your unique styles?

You can increase by adding different packaging. Or getting great accounts that will move your beer. (Not sure if this works as the answer, this might be more of a production question.)

HOWLING MUTT BREWING CO.

205 N Cedar St
Denton, TX 76201

Justin Reed

Typically, how much beer do you guys produce in an average year?

We make about 100bbls per year.

What's your favorite food to eat with beer and why?

Favorite food with beer has to be tacos because the spice makes everything nice and really compliments the hops.

About how much does it cost to open a brewery?

A nano brewery like ours cost around $150,000 to open.

In your opinion, if you were opening a brewery today what is the best BBL size to start with and why?

We chose a one bbl system because we wanted to serve our beer but we also want to serve beers from our friends who had breweries around Texas. Personally we like the decision we made.

What are today's worst beer trends?

No trend is a bad beer trend. Beer is subjective and should be appreciated as such. People like what they like and that's that

What separates breweries that don't make it in this business from the ones that do?

People like to try weird beer, but when it's a hard day you just want something that will make you relax. Overthinking the product in an industry that's supposed to make you relax seems like an oxymoron

When you first opened the brewery, what was the biggest obstacle? What advice would you give someone thinking about opening a brewery to avoid some of the pitfalls you experienced?

The biggest obstacle in opening a brewery is the permits and licenses. You will find when starting a brewery that the people making the laws know very little about your product or customers which can be very frustrating.

What beers are you best known for and why?

Our brewery specializes in a good time and it shows. We love our beer but we offer way more than that; live music, liquor infused treats, cider, wine, and craft beer. We like to make beer and we also like to give Denton a break from the daily grind.

What sets your brewery apart from most others?

We brew what we want to brew and that's what makes it special. We sit together and think about what's appealing to us and we run with it.

How do you reach beyond the hardcore beer drinkers and into the general public to sell your beer?

Always brew something light and easy and use that as gateway to better things.

What's the style most fun to brew?

IPAs are great because the hop aroma during the boil can't be beat.

When coming out with a new brew, how much experimentation do you do before you say it's ready for production?

When we brew something new we try it a small pilot system before we scale it up.

What style of beer is your best seller and why do you think that is?

Our best seller is the strawberry blonde. Probably because its light and has a low abv so you can drink all night with your friends without getting obliterated.

How important is IBU when it comes to picking out a beer? Do customers need to pay attention to it?

Most customers don't pay attention to IBUs. In the year that we have been open I think I've been asked twice what the IBUs for a beer were. We gladly have that information available but it doesn't usually affect our day to day operation.

HUMBLE ABODE BREWING

1620 E. Houston Ave
Spokane, WA 99217

Matt Gilbreath

Typically, how much beer do you guys produce in an average year?

150bbls

How much beer do you personally consume on an average workday?

1-2 pints maybe less

About how much does it cost to open a brewery?

That depends

Do you think a new brewery should serve food or just beer?

Just beer

IRON TREE RESTAURANT & FUNKY TOWN BREWERY

37 Costello Ave,
Florissant, CO 80816

Jocelyn Albrizzi

What year did you open and typically, how much beer do you guys make in a year?

The restaurant opened in 2017 and the brewery addition was in 2018 520 barrels a year

How much beer do you personally consume on an average workday?

Roughly 5 beers

What's your favorite food to eat with beer and why?

So it depends on our mood and what will pair best with it. For example we like our Pink Haze (raspberry berliner weisse) with chicken and waffles, our Groovy Golden Ale with our beer cheese burger with fries, our Far Out Milk Stout with a cheesecake or our Blurred Lines Hazy IPA with a chicken fried steak. What it really comes down to is if the beer is sour then you would want something more salty and creamy like chicken and waffles, yeasty you would want something like a burger, or smooth you would want something like fried pickles. We are super passionate about beer and food so that was a loaded question for us!

About how much does it cost to open a brewery?

We have a nano brewery so our production is very small scale. It costed us around 50k for equipment, cooler and basement remodel.

In your opinion, if you were opening a brewery today what is the best BBL size to start with and why?

We would say more of a 5 barrel because the labor doesn't incremental per barrel. So what we have learned is the less you produce the more it costs.

When you first opened the brewery, what was the biggest obstacle? What advice would you give someone thinking about opening a brewery to avoid some pitfalls you experienced?

The flow of the space and anticipated demand vs actual demand. Get everything you are going to need upfront so you do not have to continue building while you are brewing. Also, set up the climate controls for fermenting.

What separates breweries that don't make it in this business from the ones that do?

Everything has a cost. I don't think many breweries factor in the cost of everything it takes to make the beer. For example If you sell Crowlers you need to add the cost of the can, lid, and label into the price. The brewery must also factor in the cost of labor, electricity and water. The ambiance is also very important. The beer can be amazing but if there is no where to sit or the atmosphere is not enjoyable then your guests will not want to stay. Everyone wants to be happy and have a good time... your space and the vibe should amplify your beer and the experience. A brewery also needs to limit their ego and appeal to customers. If you're in a market where sour beers are big then you better start brewing some sours. Big IPA area you better have some IPAs on tap. We have 16 taps that include IPAs such as a Hazy, English, and a regular IPA. We have a raspberry berliner weisse, a golden ale, a milk stout, a brown ale, etc. We are here for the guests and our community and those people and their opinions are what can make your business sink or swim.

How did you first discover craft beer and what made you want to enter the business?

A very expensive habit haha. We love yeast and all the things you can do with it. We love the complexity and the challenge of brewing. We also love drinking beer! Food and beer are our lives and what better reason than to intertwine the both of them.

What beer would you brew if cost, production, and sales were no object?

Hazy IPA, barrel aged stouts, and a Mexican hot chocolate beer.

Do you think a new brewery should serve food or just beer?

Thats a hard question. It depends on the persons passion and what they enjoy doing. Marrying a restaurant to a brewery was very tough but we absolutely love it and wouldn't have done it any other way. You can also sell more beer with food so it creates great price points.

Being Culinary Institute grads we believe food was meant for beer and vis-versa. Theres nothing like a a beer cheese pretzel or a burger with a cold pint.

What beer is your brewery best known for and why?

Our Blurred Lines Hazy IPA because its approachable to all and IPAs are the most sold craft beer in America.

End of a long brew day, what are you drinking?

Our Groovy Golden Ale or a Moon Walker Wit.

INVENTORS BREWPUB

435 N Lake St
Port Washington, WI 53074

Adam Draeger
Owner/Brewer

Typically, how much beer do you guys produce in an average year?

110bbls

How much beer do you personally consume on an average workday?

1-2beers

What's your favorite food to eat with beer and why?

bretzeln, good German Gemutlichkeit!

About how much does it cost to open a brewery?

$1M, unless you are talented and thrifty and have friends that donate time and materials for free, then you can do it for magnitudes cheaper

Do you think a new brewery should serve food or just beer?

Food is like air. Unless you are a production brewery without a taproom, food is the responsible thing to offer to your patrons.

In your opinion, if you were opening a brewery today what is the best BBL size to start with and why?

10bbl for a pub brewery. I cannot answer this question for a packaging brewer.

What are today's worst beer trends?

Milkshake beers are very sweet and not beer-like, likewise hard seltzers are not even close to craft beer but have worked their way into many craft breweries.

What separates breweries that don't make it in this business from the ones that do?

A commitment to staff, customers and the culture/atmosphere that binds the two together.

In the past few years we have seen a massive surge in the popularity of Hazy IPA's and Sours, what do you believe the next popular beer style will be?

Craft Lagers have also been part of the Hazy IPA and sour surge. Hazy IPA's derailed my prediction but IPA's aren't going anywhere and I think some stronger versions of classic American IPA flavors will become more prominent: piney and catty. We already went down the grapefruit IPA craze a few years back. It's time for Spruce IPA's to make a run!

When you first opened the brewery, what was the biggest obstacle? What advice would you give someone thinking about opening a brewery to avoid some of the pitfalls you experienced?

Good resource management of time and money. Both are very scarce when starting your own place, so you have to be diligent with your allocations.

What beers are you best known for and why?

PW Golden Ale, Edison IPA, Lemonardo da Vinci, Flughosen Berlinerweiss. Beers that have been asked for again and again by name.

What sets your brewery apart from most others?

Our building is located on Lake Michigan with a great view and is in the American Legion Hall. This hall is the former bottlewashing building from Old Port Brewery which began it's brewing roots on this very site in 1847. One of the surface things that makes us one-of-a-kind, there are many little things that our fans like to discover that keep us unique in other ways as well.

How do you decide on new beers to brew?

We like to gauge our audience and use social media to garner ideas for beers or names for beers.

What are the biggest reasons for the continual growth of craft breweries?

If you are only served bread and water, you might want to explore other flavors. Some people will always drink Budmiloors, but we continue to see steady increase of people who like to grow and stretch themselves flavor wise.

What are the biggest obstacles to continued craft beer growth?

Local and state governments have the ability to nurture or stunt our industries growth. I hope there are enough people that will continue to fight for what they believe in.

What are the biggest problems you run into in producing beer?

For us particularly, it would be capacity on a nano-brewery.

How do you reach beyond the hardcore beer drinkers and into the general public to sell your beer?

Word of mouth is the best form of advertising. Only their friends can convince them to try something as foreign as an Amber Ale. ;)

How did you first discover craft beer and what made you want to enter the business?

I fell in love with brewpubs. I was at the Angelic Brewpub in Madison, WI and asked the bartender where "else" I could get this beer, and they answered, "nowhere, just here" that struck a chord with me that Macro produced beer couldn't.

How do you attempt to increase beer production while still staying true to both your brand and your unique styles?

NA

What's the style most fun to brew?

My favorite answer to this famous question is, "which pasta shape is the most fun to boil?" What I mean is that brewing is a process-driven activity, all the beer recipes nearly the exact same when ran through a consistent process. If anybody tells you differently, taste a flight of their different beers and if they they are all good, they will agree with my statement.

What beer would you brew if cost, production, and sales were no object?

Lagers.

Is there a popular beer you make that you just don't really like but everyone else loves?

Ozaukee Wheat is our German-style Hefeweizen. I don't hate it, I need to be in the mood for one. We can't keep in house.

End of a long brew day, what are you drinking?

Craft lagers or Sours.

How do you feel the internet has changed the way the craft brewing industry operates?

With Untappd, Ratebeer, Beeradvocate, etc it seems very easy for fans to share and brag upon beers. I can only imagine how it used to be a lot harder to spread the word.

What's the real difference between a Porter and a Stout?

I like my porters to lack roast character and instead have a cocoa note. My stouts need to have a roast character in them otherwise I'll call it a porter.

How important is IBU when it comes to picking out a beer? Do customers need to pay attention to it?

IBU's used to the measuring stick in the early 2000's but now I don't see people caring as much as long as the flavor of the beer is good.

JACK PINE BREWERY

15593 Edgewood Dr
Baxter, MN 56401

Patrick Sundberg

What year did you open and typically, how much beer do you guys make in a year?

Jack Pine opened it's doors in January of 2013. Our first year we brewed 234 barrels. We've grown to about 1600 barrels a year in 2019.

How much beer do you personally consume on an average workday?

I'll have a few samples during the day if there's something that needs a QA taste, if there's a barrel to be sampled, or if we have any warm-aged beer that needs to be evaluated. We don't really drink much during the day, but there's often a shift pint or a beer to share between the brewers near the end of the day.

What's your favorite food to eat with beer and why?

I love caramel cheesecake with a malty IPA. The contrast between sweet and bitter is amazing and the carbonation cleanses the palette so each bite of cheesecake is like the first.

About how much does it cost to open a brewery?

That could be a book upon itself. It really depends on size and scope of the brewery as well as local regulations.

In your opinion, if you were opening a brewery today what is the best BBL size to start with and why?

Start large enough to keep your tanks barely filled to keep up with demand. That will vary widely with your consumer base and competition.

When you first opened the brewery, what was the biggest obstacle? What advice would you give someone thinking about opening a brewery to avoid some pitfalls you experienced?

The largest obstacle was city zoning. We were the first brewery within 60 miles since prohibition. Taprooms were only recently allowed by the state and our city had no clue what a brewery taproom looked like and had no idea how to fit it into their zoning.

What separates breweries that don't make it in this business from the ones that do?

Business sense. Beer is fun and it's something that you can get very passionate about, but at the end of the day it's still a business.

How did you first discover craft beer and what made you want to enter the business?

I found craft beer in college and started brewing my own. I entered many homebrewing competitions, won a number of medals, because a beer judge, put together a business plan and started a brewery. Long story short, I'm a homebrewer turned pro.

What beer would you brew if cost, production, and sales were no object?

I already do that. We have a 1 barrel pilot system and 24 beers on tap, so I can really put nearly anything on tap that I'd like to brew. I do, however, have an affinity for traditional sour beers and just don't have the patience (or space) to do them well. I've had far too many fantastic Flanders Reds to try to do my own. I don't feel I could do them justice.

Do you think a new brewery should serve food or just beer?

Just beer, but that's just my opinion. I have zero experience in the hospitality industry, so I had no interest in trying to build a kitchen. I'd rather stick with what I know and do that really well than be average at two things.

What beer is your brewery best known for and why?

Our longest running unique beer is our Vengeance! Jalapeno Cream Ale. We've brewed that pretty much year round since our first year. Our base cream ale provides a wonderfully neutral backdrop for the fresh cut jalapenos. It has enough spice to be evident, but not enough to overpower. There's a good balance there and the aroma is amazing! It just came together really well. Well enough that we were able to take a bronze medal in the GABF for it.

End of a long brew day, what are you drinking?

I tend to drink to the season or the weather. On a cold winter day, I love barrel aged stouts. At the peak of summer, a clean pilsner hits the spot. But honestly, if you hand me a beer at the end of the day, I won't turn it down.

JACKSON STREET BREWING

607 5th St
Sioux City, IA 51101

Dave Winslow
Brewer/Owner

What year did you open and typically, how much beer do you guys make in a year?

2015. 250-300 barrels

How much beer do you personally consume on an average workday?

1-2 pints...only samples while working

What's your favorite food to eat with beer and why?

Pizza or a burger

About how much does it cost to open a brewery?

Too much. We started for less than $80K but should have spent around $200K to start correctly

In your opinion, if you were opening a brewery today what is the best BBL size to start with and why?

3-10 bbl to cut your teeth and be nimble. Market saturation is real, and being much bigger than this is going to mean your beers will sit for a while and will be brewing new beers infrequently

When you first opened the brewery, what was the biggest obstacle? What advice would you give someone thinking about opening a brewery to avoid some pitfalls you experienced?

Money and knowledge. Do your research. There's lots of good info out there now, more than when we started

What separates breweries that don't make it in this business from the ones that do?

Opening a brewery just because it would be fun or cool often leads to eventual closing. It has to be a passion driven by smart business sense, and careful spending of money.

How did you first discover craft beer and what made you want to enter the business?

Right after college we fell in love with hoppy pale ales from Sierra Nevada, Boulevard, Summit Brewing and Dogfish Head. We wanted to be around beer all the time and were the first in our medium sized market to go for a brewery post 2000

What beer would you brew if cost, production, and sales were no object?

Oktoberfest all year

Do you think a new brewery should serve food or just beer?

If you can do food with a small kitchen team this would be ideal due to overhead costs…better yet food trucks

What beer is your brewery best known for and why?

Sioux City Sour or barrel aged stouts. They get people excited and hopefully we are making them somewhat balanced rather than the shock value some breweries go for in beers to get attention these days.

End of a long brew day, what are you drinking?

5-6% ABV West Coast IPA, or a well made German Lager.

KENNAY FARMS DISTILLING

416 Lincoln Hwy
Rochelle, IL 61068

Aubrey Quinn
Marketing and Logistics

Typically, how much beer do you guys make in a year?

We have only been open for one year so don't have a lot of data. Last year
we offered 21 different beers.

How much beer do you personally consume on an average workday?

Usually just one or two to unwind after the week on a Friday.

What's your favorite food to eat with beer and why?

Pretzels or nuts. Salt!

About how much does it cost to open a brewery?

Would certainly depend on the size.

What are today's worst beer trends?

I don't care for the peanut butter beers but they seem to be popular.

When you first opened the brewery, what was the biggest obstacle? What advice would you give someone thinking about opening a brewery to avoid some pitfalls you experienced?

Planning the right space and equipment. Know your audience and don't try to be too trendy or fancy.

How do you decide on new beers to brew?

Keep an eye on the market and listen to what your customers want.

How did you first discover craft beer and what made you want to enter the business?

We are first a distillery but thought beer would attract a wider clientele.

What beer would you brew if cost, production, and sales were no object?

I like Hefeweizens.

Does glassware really make a difference?

To the customer it does and that is what matters.

What beer is your brewery best known for and why?

Mother Hen and Buttermilk are the two best sellers. They are made with local hops.

End of a long brew day, what are you drinking?

Mother Hen Hefeweizen is my favorite.

KNOX COUNTY BREWING CO.

2900 W Main St
Galesburg, IL 61401

Matthew Hansen

Typically, how much beer do you guys make in a year?

We are really small. We serve a county with around 50k people.

How much beer do you personally consume on an average workday?

Not very much at all. I may consume about 12-24 ounces a week. I'm a bit of a health nut and a runner. While I love beer, I allow myself 12-24 ounces a weeks. Of course if I'm traveling I love trying other beers out there.

What's your favorite food to eat with beer and why?

Actually, I don't typically like drinking beer and eating food at the same time. That said, I do love to eat cheese with good old world style beers

About how much does it cost to open a brewery?

Ah, man this one is all over the page. This depends on your goal. In the US we seem to have a cultural value of starting with what could be a finished product. Rather than doing the only the necessary to get off the ground, and then grow into the brewery and piece it together as we go. We did not plan with best case scenario in mind. We live within a vulnerable economy, especially here within the rural MidWest. To top it off we live in a country that believes "big or growing economy" equates to healthy economy, and that simply is not the case. We were told it would cost us upwards of $500k to open our brewery. With a rebel's attitude we set out to do it with $150k. And we did. But we sacrificed a lot, and I believe that is the equation one should look for, "what can you sacrifice without sacrificing quality and flavor?" We spent very little on our actual brew system, we rely on a lot of manual strength to do what we do. We only opened up to a capacity that allows us to run the brewery with our family only, so we have not employee costs. This allows us to keep a low over head, low start up cost, and yet purchase 100% local ingredients. Within the first 18 months of our opening we have been able to pay 30% of our debt off. We haven't taken on any new debt and have paid everything with cash. And we won "Best of the Best" craft beer in Knox County and "Best of the Best" environment to enjoy a craft beer within our first 12 months of opening. All of this has allowed us to thrive within this rural community even in the midst of the Covid pandemic. My point is, one does not have to sacrifice quality and environment for low-cost start up.

What are today's worst beer trends?

In my opinion, the fact that there are trends is the worst beer trend. I hate fads, they lack intellectual integrity. I love beers that represent a context and culture, rather than beers and styles that take on the principles of fast fashion. It's kind of like when hipsters made brussel sprouts popular. How the hell can a food be a fad, and yet it is. I think that says more about our society than it does the beer. Look at places that are still producing the best the beer in the world - Belgium and Germany. Don't get me wrong - I'm all for innovation and I love change, but when the "craft BEER" world begins to play around with equating things like "hard seltzer" to "CRAFT beer", we are more about bottom lines than we are craft, and that is often the danger zone of following trends.

When you first opened the brewery, what was the biggest obstacle? What advice would you give someone thinking about opening a brewery to avoid some pitfalls you experienced?

(1) Walk in with the attitude and knowledge that you don't know it all. I hired some consultants. But these consultants were vetted, and part of a brewing company that we had known for years. We trusted them. We also spotted out breweries that exemplified the quality and values we did and got to know them, and learned from them.

(2) Trust your gut, this is one that seems to be contradictory to the point I just mentioned, but you probably know your context better than them. For example, one of our consultants suggested we go for a 10-15 bbl brew system. On one hand that would have been more debt, on the other hand, something inside of me knew that was too big for our context. We didn't plan on brewing for anything larger than our county. Find the balance between your gut and the experts.

(3) Also, be honest about what you need versus what you want. What is the least amount you need to spend and still accomplish what you want to accomplish. Be honest about it. Often times your first year or two of survival is more about how much you don't spend at the beginning than about how much you make.

(4) Brew the beers you want to brew. If you are a small local brewery represent your locality. We do this two ways - one, I love old world beers, so that's what I brew the most of. And it shows, it's what I love, because they are our best beers. I'm not a lager drinker, and while I do like IPAs, I'm kind of over it, unless they are big and bold. So I don't brew session IPAs, if people want a session IPA, I'll recommend another brewery. We are not afraid to do that. We don't try to own the market, we try to brew what we love the best. So, while the majority of the beers are our favorite types of beers, we will dedicate a tap or two to the local trend - IPA, Lager, etc...brew what you love because it will show. Two, we represent our locality by brewing with only Illinois grown hops and only

midwestern malts. One on hand this creates some limitations, but on the other it ignites creativity - how do we brew old world beers with what we have locally available? That's the fun part - figuring that equation out.

How do you decide on new beers to brew?

We brew what we love to brew. As I mentioned above, we dedicate a few taps to the norms or trends - IPAs, lagers, etc... but then we have a range of Old World recipes that we have worked out, that range in ABV. Our goal is that our menu represents the range in ABV and flavors. So, "we brew next", whatever will replace what we seem to be running out of.

How did you first discover craft beer and what made you want to enter the business?

My gateway into the craft beer world begins with this simple phrase from me, "I don't like beer." That's right, those words come out of my mouth. I said that to a friend of mine, and thankfully, he refused to take me at face value. He insisted I had just not had the right beer yet. He then asked me a series of questions and ordered a beer for me. I was amazed. Then a craft beer brewery opened up down the hall from our gym, Hops and Grains, and I was amazed at the range of profiles and characteristics within these beers. Next some friends of our were opening a larger brewery, which is where I was introduced to Old World beers, and we fell in love. From there we began to tour and visit small local breweries every time we traveled. We fell in love with the culture as much as we fell in love with the beer itself. It was so inspiring to see these women and men of craft create something like beer as a conduit for community creation and values. It was a world we longed for and could relate to. As far as opening up a brewery, that was never in the plans for us. We moved to the rural midwest as a way to fall off the map. We are from Austin, Texas, and we needed a break. The work we did in Austin wasn't going to work here - at least not as a way to create an income. We begin to imagine what it would be like to open a brewery that rested on the foundational-values of the other work we had done in the big city. Could high quality beer become a conduit for things bigger than beer? We believed the answer was, YES! So we rolled the dice. Worst case scenario - we fail. But, our motto has always been, that we would rather fail trying something we wanted to try than live the rest of our lives wondering, "what if."

What beer would you brew if cost, production, and sales were no object?

There is no beer I won't brew, if I want to brew it. I believe if you love it and you have the patience, it will work. Maybe I'm naive, but for now, it seems to work. I just brewed a 15% ABV braggot, which is currently resting in two barrels. Six-percent of the grist is a two-row malt that I smoked over maple wood. Nothing about this says it will sell well around here. A lot of tannins. Big in alcohol. Really out of the box. But I wanted to brew it. So I did. We'll see.

Does glassware really make a difference?

Maybe, but in my humble opinion, not as much as folks say. I've seen this polar extremes in two parts of the world I love - England and Belgium. In Belgium, where bottled beer is preferred, they seem to have a different glass for every beer, where in the old countryside pubs of England, a nice larger regular pint glass seems to fit almost every thing.

What beer is your brewery best known for and why?

We've been open 18 months. We are more widely praised for our Old World Beers. We have made the entire range. But to even narrow it down, our Belgium style beers seem to be our crowd favorites, and frankly we love to brew them. These past 18 months have allowed us to brew it all, and see what we liked the most. I think you will begin to see Knox County Brewing Co, begin to lean in to becoming specialists of Old World Beers, dominantly Belgian-style beers. I think they best set the tone for who we want to be as a brewery.

End of a long brew day, what are you drinking?

My wife's house made kombucha! Unless it is cold outside, then I'll drink one of our big Belgians or darks.

KELSEY CITY BREWING COMPANY

720 Park Avenue
Lake Park, FL 33403

John Hampp
Head Brewer

Typically, how much beer do you guys make in a year?

We're really about as new as you can get but the target is for us to produce about 100 barrels our first year. That will likely be about 2 styles with a few variations with each style.

How much beer do you personally consume on an average workday?

About 10 – 12 pints a week

What's your favorite food to eat with beer and why?

That is a difficult question as it depends on the beer. My favorite food with a variety of beers would have to be a wood fired Margherita pizza.

About how much does it cost to open a brewery?

For a nano-brewery like ours you can do it for less than $100k. Every piece you add to make your life as a brewer easier just adds to the price.

What are today's worst beer trends?

That is a "beauty is in the eye of the beholder" question as it relates to beer trends but for me personally is the trend of really good breweries selling out to the majors. We all do this for the passion of making beer that we like but at the end of the day you need an exit plan and when a large envelope of money is thrown at you its hard to think of what that will do to your customers and supporters. There has been a growing trend of brewery failures as the weight of the borrowed money to cover capital and O&M expenses becomes crushing and failure is unavoidable. Over capitalization has been responsible for the death of many breweries just last year and will happen more frequently with the fallout of the pandemic effects.

When you first opened the brewery, what was the biggest obstacle? What advice would you give someone thinking about opening a brewery to avoid some pitfalls you experienced?

Since we are brand new, the obvious answer is COVID-19, or any pandemic, and the shutdown of your revenue source. Our biggest obstacle was translating what we want to our contractors so they understood what we need. There are few contractors at that time who had any brewery experience in our area. You can avoid a lot of grief by communicating to your contractors with everything you can including lots of photos and drawings. The other piece of advice is the last minute costs are going to be twice what you think they will be because the clock is ticking and the need to start generating revenue is clearly in the forefront of everything you do.

How do you decide on new beers to brew?

We started as a tap house with 43 taps and still carry a large variety of beers. We started focusing on the styles of our best sellers as our first beers. We are also highly influenced by family and friends about their expectations of what they want to see on the list of a brewery when they walk in the door. After that I think about what styles I'd like to brew and then what flavors of that style are likely to catch the interest of our customers that will translate into sales. I meet with the owners and our team to get their reactions and input as well. AJ at the Brewhouse Gallery is deeply interested in the history of Kelsey City and has brought out so many points about the history of the area that have been inspirations for our beer styles and flavors. From that research I've developed the recipes to highlight a theme for each beer to tie it to the history of our area. There are some styles that I know are popular but are not my interest to make. Those I leave to the other brewers to run with.

How did you first discover craft beer and what made you want to enter the business?

That is a very long trail that started with a microbiology course in college where our project was to make beer and study yeast. There were some imports available in Florida but everything else was the majors. That started my interest in homebrewing which I still continue to this day. A buddy of mine that I met at a local brewpub decided to build a new homebrew rig and to brew at least every month. By the 4th brew we were getting 7 – 20 people showing up on brew day and we were encouraged to enter our beers into homebrew competitions. After we started getting medals in different categories we knew that we could brew good beers but had much more to learn. The desire to get into the business was quite honestly the plan to make beer more often and try new styles and experiment and understand more with the palate of ingredients that we have. I think as a brewer you never stop learning because you can never know it all. It seems like we never stop hearing about a lost style that was resurrected or yeast cultures that were isolated.

What beer would you brew if cost, production, and sales were no object?

Easy answer, lagers. Specifically Doppelbocks. We can't do decoction brews with our setup and in the postage stamp size brewery space we also can't add horizontal lagering tanks.

Does glassware really make a difference?

Absoutely. In all aspects: Cleanliness, shape, & size. I would love to have the proper glass for each style but frankly there's not enough room to store them all so you make compromises. Never compromise on cleanliness though.

What beer is your brewery best known for and why?

We are on our 7th brew at the moment and our Wheat Ale brewed with Kveik yeast has been the most popular up to date but our bohemian pilsner is likely to pass it. I love brewing with the Kveik yeast and making sure it stresses a little to throw that big pineapple aroma and flavor. Having only a few runs on the equipment we are doing what my homebrew friends know me best for, "tweaking".

End of a long brew day, what are you drinking?

I can say without hesitation that is going to be a lager. A Czech pils, a Helles, or a german pils. If I bring in homebrew to share that beer could also be a Tmave or Schwarzbier as well.

KNOTTED ROOT BREWING COMPANY

250 North Caribou St
Nederland, CO 80466

Chris Marchio
Founder & Head Brewer

Typically, how much beer do you guys produce in an average year?

Around 800 bbls per year.

How much beer do you personally consume on an average workday?

1 - 2 beers.

What's your favorite food to eat with beer and why?

I don't necessarily have a favorite. Depends on the day, sometimes it's a burger, pizza, charcuterie, spicy thai noodles.

About how much money does it cost to open a brewery?

Depends on the size of the brewery, area, rent, taproom SF, overall approach. One could open a nano brewery for probably around $10,000 - $15,000. One could open a production brewery for $2,000,000. Most breweries probably cost anywhere from $500,000 - $1,000,000 to open.

What are today's worst beer trends?

I am personally not the biggest fans of most pastry stouts. I think some can be fun, the taste's can certainly be fun and exciting, but they tend to be too sweet, thick, and chewy to be able to enjoy more than a little bit.

In the past few years we have seen a massive surge in the popularity of Hazy IPA's and Sours, what do you believe the next popular beer style will be?

I am seeing a resurgence in oak aged lagers. I really hope this is it. I also don't see Hazy IPA's going anywhere if they're done well, or sours going anywhere. Maybe tart, fruited stouts will make a come up?

When you first opened the brewery, what was the biggest obstacle? What advice would you give someone thinking about opening a brewery to avoid some of the pitfalls you experienced?

Local regulations. Make sure you know what you're doing is legal and do everything you can to work with your local community to ensure you are welcomed wherever you set up. Also, make sure you're good at this, it's competitive nowadays.

What beers are you best known for and why?

Unfiltered IPAs, fruited smoothie-style sours that we do in our own way, unfiltered lagerbier, and hopefully soon, mixed-culture fermentation ales.

What sets your brewery apart from most others?

Our location, nuanced- approach to brewing, our brewing water profile, artwork, our vibe and the people who are involved with the company.

How do you decide on new beers to brew?

Intuition and feeling.

What are the biggest reasons for the continual growth of craft breweries?

No reason, I see a decline for most breweries unfortunately.

What are the biggest obstacles to continued craft beer growth?

Right now, COVID.. but that applies to everyone. The quality of your product and how you market your beer.

What are the biggest problems you run into in producing beer?

Scheduling.

How do you reach beyond the hardcore beer drinkers and into the general public to sell your beer?

We personally don't worry about that. We just do what we do and hope people like it.

How did you first discover craft beer and what made you want to enter the business?

I stole a Prima Pils from my dad when I was like 17. I fell in love with homebrewing and didn't want to work a corporate job.

How do you attempt to increase beer production while still staying true to both your brand and your unique styles?

Through balance and sustainable growth.

What's the style most fun to brew?

I like to brew our fruited sours and IPAs. Barrel aged wild ales are the most rewarding.

Is there a popular beer you make that you just don't really like but everyone else loves?

no

End of a long brew day, what are you drinking?

Pilsners or Banquet. We're in Colorado so Coors is very local and it's a refreshing light beer.

What are a few beers that other brewers are making that you really find impressive?

Primitive in Longmont, CO... anything by Hill Farmstead in Vermont off the top of my head. There are so many that I can't list them all.

How do you feel the internet has changed the way the craft brewing industry operates?

Marketing, online beer photography and advertising, customers discussing beers, and trading.

When coming out with a new brew, how much experimentation do you try to get in before you say it's ready for production?

none.

What style of beer is your bestseller and why do you think that is?

IPA and Fruited Sour.

Does glassware really make a difference?

Depending on the style, yes.

What's the real difference between a Porter and a Stout?

Porter is lighter, drier, and a little hoppier. Stout should be more rich, roasty.

How important is IBU when it comes to picking out a beer? Do customers need to pay attention to it?

For most styles, there should be a range you hit as a brewer. As long as you're in the range, I don't think the customer really knows or cares much about them.

KALISPELL BREWING CO.

412 Main St
Kalispell, MT 59901

Amber Hogan
Director of Marketing and Events

Typically, how much beer do you guys produce in an average year?

1600 to 2000 BBLS/YR

How much beer do you personally consume on an average workday?

Everyone who works here gets one free shift beer per shift, and a free
growler fill each week. I usually have a shifty or two! (I'm the Marketing
Director, so have to drink a few to get that content for social media.)

What's your favorite food to eat with beer and why?

Soft pretzels and beer cheese. Our resident food truck makes them from scratch and they are SO good!

What are today's worst beer trends?

We have a pretty traditional line-up of mostly German lagers, so we don't chase too many fads. We will likely never add fruit to our beer, or make a Milkshake IPA, not that they are the worst, just not our style.

In the past few years we have seen a massive surge in the popularity of Hazy IPA's and Sours, what do you believe the next popular beer style will be?

We want to see lagers come back! #makebeerclearagain

When you first opened the brewery, what was the biggest obstacle? What advice would you give someone thinking about opening a brewery to avoid some of the pitfalls you experienced?

If you know anything about Montana brewing laws, nothing is easy about opening a brewery here. It took us years to get everything up to code and approved by city officials. After that, it was adjusting to the laws, which only allow breweries in the state to serve 48oz per person per day, and abide by a strict closing time of 8pm. All I would say is, if you want it bad enough, you will make it happen!

What beers are you best known for and why?

Two Ski Brewski Pilsner and Winter at Noon Dunkel. Both German lagers that we brew in the most traditional way, using a triple decoction method that most people no longer use.

What sets your brewery apart from most others?

The difference in in the decoction! Here's a bit more about that process from our website. The extra step: decoction is a time-honored brewing technique that allows sugars to be extracted from the malt more effectively. To some it's no longer necessary with today's specialty malts, but it's what gives our lagers the complexity and balance we strive for. And when your head brewer wears lederhosen while tending to the Oktoberfest mash, it's pretty obvious that his passion for the craft outweighs any inconvenience that stems from the extra effort. It's traditional, it's technical and it's time consuming. Don't think too much about it. We'll do the labor while you savor.

End of a long brew day, what are you drinking?

Two Ski Brewski Pilsner!

Does glassware really make a difference?

We certainly think so! In fact we pride ourselves on using style specific glassware. Just like the selection of hops and malt play a vital role in brewing, enjoying beer from a glass that's intended to bring out all the nuances of flavor, color, and aroma, is equally as important. Simply put, a specifically designed beer glass will enhance your experience for complete craft brew enjoyment. Plus, it's just plain fun. We're all about fun.

KANSAS CITY BIER COMPANY, LLC

310 W. 79th Street
Kansas City, MO 64114

Stephen R. Holle
Managing Partner

Typically, how much beer do you guys make in a year?

IN 2019 WE SHIPPED 16,500 BBLS.

How much beer do you personally consume on an average workday?

THAT IS HARD TO SAY BECAUSE I AM
SAMPLING BIER THROUGHOUT THE DAY FOR QUALITY
ASSURANCE AND FOR COMPARISONS TO OTHER
COMMERCIAL BREWERS.

What's your favorite food to eat with beer and why?

THE BEER SELECTED TO PAIR WITH FOOD DEPENDS ON WHAT I AM EATING. BUT, THE FIRST PAIRING THAT COMES TO MIND IS PIZZA. PIZZA IS A FAVORITE FOOD AND BECAUSE IT IS SALTY AND GREASY, A COLD THIRST-QUENCHING BIER MAKES A GREAT COMPANION. OUR PILS OR HELLES LAGER ARE A GREAT MATCH BECAUSE EITHER BEER QUENCHES THE SALT INDUCED THIRST, AND THE HOPS CUT THROUGH THE GREASE TO CLEAN THE PALLET.

About how much does it cost to open a brewery?

THE COST TO OPEN A BREWERY DEPENDS ON YOUR GOALS. IF A BREWER WANTS A SMALL NANO-BREWERY, ESPECIALLY A SMALL DRAUGHT ONLY TASTING ROOM, THAT COULD BE ACCOMPLISHED FOR UNDER $100,000. IF THE PLAN IS FOR A LARGER BREWERY THAT DISTRIBUTES WHOLESALE (LIKE KC BIER CO) SERVING PACKAGED BIER AND KEGS, THE COST IS IN THE MILLIONS OF DOLLARS.

What are today's worst beer trends?

HARD SELTZERS. WHILE HARD SELTZERS ARE NOT BEER, THEY GET LUMPED INTO THE BEER CATEGORY BECAUSE THEY ARE TYPICALLY PRODUCED BY BREWERS AND DISTRIBUTED BY BEER WHOLESALERS. BUT THE GENESIS OF THE HARD SELTZER TREND CAN BE TRACED BACK TO THE CREATION OF LIGHT BEER BY THE US BEER INDUSTRY. FOR DECADES LIGHT BEER PRODUCERS HAVE BEEN SELLING LIGHT BEER BY TELLING CONSUMERS THAT NON-LIGHT BEER MAKES DRINKERS FAT, FILLS THEM UP, OR GIVES THEM A "BITTER BEER FACE". THEN THE CRAFT BEER INDUSTRY CAME ALONG AND STARTED MAKING BLAND BASE BEERS FLAVORED WITH FRUIT TO ATTRACT THE LIGHT BEER DRINKER. THE END RESULT ARE LOW-CALORIE HARD SELTZER MADE WITH NEUTRAL ALCOHOL SPIRITS AND FLAVORED WITH FRUIT OR ARTIFICIAL FLAVORS. SO, MANY CRAFT BREWERIES HAVE DEVOLVED INTO CHASING THE

SAME CONSUMER TRENDS, WHICH 20 YEARS AGO THEY FOUGHT AGAINST.

When you first opened the brewery, what was the biggest obstacle? What advice would you give someone thinking about opening a brewery to avoid some pitfalls you experienced?

WHILE COMMISSIONING ANY MANUFACTURING OR FOOD PROCESSING ENTERPRISE IS EXPENSIVE AND COMPLICATED, I WISH I HAD SPENT MORE TIME UNDERSTANDING THE INTRICACIES OF WHOLESALE BEER DISTRIBUTION. WHOLESALERS AND RETAILERS HAVE COMMON, BUT ALSO DIFFERENT, CONCERNS AND CHALLENGES THAN A SUPPLIER. THERE ARE DECADES OLD STANDARDS FOR WORKING WITH WHOLESALERS TO SUPPORT THERE OPERATIONS , OF WHICH I WAS UNAWARE. UNDERSTANDING DISTRIBUTION IS EXTREMELY IMPORTANT FOR ACHIEVING SUCCESS AND GROWTH.

How do you decide on new beers to brew?

WE FOCUS ON A NARROW NICHE BY BREWING TRADITIONAL GERMAN-STYLE BEER. WE HAVE RESISTED MAKING ONE OFF BRANDS OR THE FLAVOR OF THE MONTH. WE STARTED WITH POPULAR TRADITIONAL GERMAN STYLES AND KEEP EXPLORING NEW GERMAN STYLES WHEN THE TIME IS RIGHT. WE SOMETIMES PUT AN AMERICAN TWIST ON A GERMAN STYLE OR VICE VERSA, BUT WE ALWAYS STAY CONNECTED TO GERMAN BREWING TRADITIONS BY USING IMPORTED GERMAN MALT AND HOPS AND FOLLOWING TRADITIONAL BREWING METHODS.

How did you first discover craft beer and what made you want to enter the business?

I AM 62 YEARS OLD AND I HAVE ALWAYS BEEN AN ADVENTUROUS BEER DRINKER SINCE I WAS OLD ENOUGH TO DRINK. I STUDIED GERMAN IN HIGH SCHOOL AND COLLEGE

AND STUDIED ABROAD, SO I WAS EXPOSED TO GERMAN AND OTHER EUROPEAN STYLES BEFORE THE CRAFT BEER MOVEMENT STARTED IN THE US. AS CRAFT BEERS BECAME MORE AVAILABLE, I WAS EAGER TO EXPLORE THEM ALL.

What beer would you brew if cost, production, and sales were no object?

I REALLY DON'T THINK THERE IS ANY STYLE WE ARE PROHIBITED FROM BREWING THAT WE WOULD WANT TO BREW BECAUSE OF COST. WE USE VERY EXPENSIVE, TIME-CONSUMING METHODS TO MAKE TRADITIONAL GERMAN LAGERS INCLUDING DECOCTION MASHING, TWO TANK FERMENTATION AND CONDITIIONG, NATURAL CARBONATION, LONG COLD LAGERING PERIODS, AS WELL AS IMPORTING ALL OF OUR MALT AND HOPS. HOWEVER, THERE IS ALWAYS A BETTER PIECE OF EQUIPMENT A BREWER DESIRES, AND FOR ME, I WISH WE HAD THE SPACE TO CREATE AN OPEN FERMENTATION CELLAR TO BREW OUR HEFEWEIZEN. SOME DAY.

Does glassware really make a difference?

KC BIER CO HAS STYLE-APPROPRIATE GLASSWARE FOR ALL OF OUR STYLES, AND THE BEER WE SERVE IN OUR TASTING ROOM IS ALWAYS SOLD IN THE APPROPRIATE GLASS. THE TYPE OF GLASSWARE IS NOT AS IMPORTANT AS THE SIMPLE FACT THAT BEER SHOULD BE ENJOYED FROM A GLASS TO RELEASE AROMAS AND ENHANCE FLAVOR. FURTHERMORE, BEER HAS THE UNIQUE CAPACITY AMONG ALCOHOLIC BEVERAGES TO PRODUCE A STABLE FOAM HEAD. WHAT BETTER WAY TO PRESENT THE BEAUTY AND UNIQUENESS OF BEER THAN TO CROWN IT WITH A LUSCIOUS CROWN OF FOAM. MOREOVER, WHEN BEER IS SERVED IN THE APPROPRIATE GLASS IT SHOWS THE CONSUMER THAT THE RETAILER RESPECTS THE QUALITY OF THE BEVERAGE AND WANTS TO MAXIMIZE THE DRINKING EXPERIENCE OF THEIR CUSTOMER. A WINE DRINKER WOULD NEVER ACCEPT A

GLASS OF WINE SERVED IN A COCKTAIL SHAKER PINT, SO WHY SHOULD THE BEER CONSUMER? HOWEVER, I AM NOT A BEER GLASS SNOB. THERE ARE MANY TIMES, LIKE AT A TAILGATE OR AFTER A SOFTBALL GAME, WHEN I WILL DRINK OUT OF THE BOTTLE. MY MOTO HAS ALWAYS BEEN: GLASSWARE IS MADE FOR BEER, NOT BEER FOR GLASSWARE.

What beer is your brewery best known for and why?

A BROWN MUNICH-STYLE LAGER, DUNKEL, IS BY FAR OUR BEST SELLER. ALTHOUGH WE MAKE AWARD-WINNING GOLDEN LAGERS, I THINK MANY CRAFT BEER DRINKERS HAVE A BIAS AGAINST PALE LAGERS BECAUSE THEY WRONGLY ASSOCIATE THEM WITH CHEAP, BLAND DOMESTICS. DUNKEL HAS A RICH MALT CHARACTER OF TOASTED BREAD AND CARAMEL, BUT YET IS SMOOTH AND REFRESHING. DUNKEL LOOKS MORE "CRAFTY" THAN A GOLDEN LAGER, SO IT WAS THE FIRST BEER RETAILERS PUT ON TAP. PEOPLE TRIED IT AND LIKED ITS FLAVOR AND APPROACHABILITY. PLUS, THE DEEP BROWN COLOR LOOKS EXOTIC WHEN THE DRINKER IS HOLDING THE BEER IN THEIR HAND.

End of a long brew day, what are you drinking?

HELLES, A MUNICH-STYLE GOLD LAGER. IT HAS A RICH CLEAN MALT CHARACTER, BUT IS FLAVORFUL, EASY-DRINKING, AND TOTALLY REFRESHING

KOI POND BREWING CO.

1107 Falls Rd
Rocky Mount, NC 27804

Joshua T. Parvin
Co-Owner

Typically, how much beer do you guys make in a year?

220 bbls

How much beer do you personally consume on an average workday?

A few ounces at most for quality control as part of the job.   Otherwise, I
may have 1 or 2 beers if I am eating dinner at home.

What's your favorite food to eat with beer and why?

Pizza. Is there a better food to eat with anything?! The variety of pizza out there allows for endless options for pairing with craft beer.

About how much does it cost to open a brewery?

I am not sure. We lease our premises and the brewing equipment is part of that lease. Although I have been an employee of KPBC since we opened in Jan 2016, I did not become a partner until Sept 2018. I do know we saved a lot of money on legal fees since my partners are lawyers. That certainly helped.

What are today's worst beer trends?

The market is oversaturated with IPAs that wreck the palate. If I want to eat hops, I'll go to a hops farm. Just my opinion and for the record, I do like IPAs. Also, I don't' know why everyone is always obsessed with newness. I even have to reign in my head brewer sometimes. 1 or 2 new beers per month is more than plenty. I am a firm believer in our flagship beers. If flagship beers are done well, consumers will come back for those beers time after time. Our consumers know when they walk in the door of our taproom and see something familiar on the tap list, it will taste the same as it did last year and it will taste the same next year. There is an inherent comfort in knowing what a beer tastes like before ordering. Sure, you can get a taste of "the next best thing", but sometimes (maybe most of the time...) you just want something familiar!!

How do you decide on new beers to brew?

I give my brewer full license to come up with new recipes as long as he keeps the new beers to 1 or 2 per month. He will let me know what he has in mind and I will usually give the okay as long as we do not need one of our flagships brewed.

How did you first discover craft beer and what made you want to enter the business?

I went to school in Colorado in the late 90's. I didn't care or know anything about "craft' beer at the time, but that is where I was introduced to Fat Tire by New Belgium for the first time. From there, although I drank mostly cheaper "big beer" since I was on a student's budget, I would usually make an effort to try new things. I remember a restaurant called Old Chicago. They had a menu with 120 or so different beers. Whenever I went there to eat, I would usually try one or two beers I had never had before. I have continued to do that since. I call it market research!

What beer would you brew if cost, production, and sales were no object?

10 Coin Day is our Belgian Golden Strong Ale and my favorite beer we make!

Does glassware really make a difference?

Not in my opinion. I have used all different kinds of glasses and never paid attention to, or noticed, the difference in taste. I have never had a customer tell me I am using the wrong type of glass. When I am at home, I use a regular pint glass for all beer.

What beer is your brewery best known for and why?

Our brewers do really well with Belgians and Saisons, but I think we are best known for VooDoo Wit, our Blood Orange Witbier. Light enough to drink year round and refreshing enough to keep you coming back for more. Goes well with any food.

End of a long brew day, what are you drinking?

Our own Falls Road Golden Kolsch. Light, crisp, and very refreshing!

LAUNCH PAD BREWERY

884 S Buckley Rd
Aurora, CO 80017

David Levesque
Founder/Brewmaster

Typically, how much beer do you guys make in a year?

We produced 800 barrels of beer in 2019 and are shooting for 1000 barrels in 2020

How much beer do you personally consume on an average workday?

I would say I average about 5 or 6 beers daily, maybe more since COVID 19, LOL

What's your favorite food to eat with beer and why?

I would say that I love Italian food while drinking beer, the acidity balances the malt and hops for me.

About how much does it cost to open a brewery?

I started Launch Pad brewery with $350,000. We started as a nano brewery on a 1 barrel brewhouse with plastic conicals, produced 305 barrels our first year.

What are today's worst beer trends?

Brut IPAS and if you consider Hard Seltzer beer, I don't, but Hard Seltzers.

When you first opened the brewery, what was the biggest obstacle? What advice would you give someone thinking about opening a brewery to avoid some pitfalls you experienced?

Getting Funding, finding a bank to back your financing needs is probably the most difficult thing to open a brewery. We have grown slowly and been able to withstand pitfalls in the industry, so my advice would be to take it slowly and be comfortable in your decisions to grow.

How do you decide on new beers to brew?

We get a lot of inspiration from drinking and eating, we come up with some of our best ideas when we are relaxed and free minded.

How did you first discover craft beer and what made you want to enter the business?

I was in the military stationed in Minot ND and there was no craft beer there, then transferred to Buckley AFB in Denver CO and that's when I was introduced to craft beer. A local brewery taught me how to home brew and just feel in love with the craft and the art of creating a delicious beer.

What beer would you brew if cost, production, and sales were no object?

We really don't worry about cost at launch pad, we try to produce the highest quality product everyday, so we have created multiple beers that were fairly expensive. Our most expensive beer to date was probably our Pecan pie Russian Imperial stout aged in whisky barrels, it turns out pecans are extremely expensive.

Does glassware really make a difference?

It definitely does. We do multiple sensory events and trial by putting the same beer in different glassware, it is crazy to see how people pick up and different flavors and aromas.

What beer is your brewery best known for and why?

Probably our Piggyback Rides juicy IPA, it's an east coast style juicy IPA that is hopped with fun tropical hop profile.

End of a long brew day, what are you drinking?

Whiskey, Scotch, or Gin and tonic. After drinking beer all day long I like to switch it up to relax. Now if it is a beer it would most likely be a Belgian Quad with cherries.

In the past few years we have seen a massive surge in the popularity of Hazy IPA's and Sours, what do you believe the next popular beer style will be?

I think we are going to see a swing back to clean, clear, crisp beer like lagers and west coast IPAs. Maybe with the use of more non traditional and experimental hops.

LABYRINTH FORGE BREWING COMPANY

Portland, OR

Dylan
Owner

Typically, how much beer do you guys produce in an average year?

We have a unique business model. Although we are a brewery, our system, currently, is very small (1/2 bbl). We don't brew very often yet. Therefore, our actual production is currently very low. I estimate we do about 1 bbl a year at the moment. We contract out most of our beer to other breweries with extra capacity. This enabled us to "produce" 30 bbls last year (our first year) and we're on track to "produce" 50+ bbl this year.

How much beer do you personally consume on an average workday?

I drive doing deliveries in the evenings, so I don't drink a beer everyday. On average, I would say I probably drink 2-3 beers per week unless there is a social gathering, then it can go to 5-7.

What's your favorite food to eat with beer and why?

I eat just about anything with beer. Surprisingly, even sweet stuff goes pretty well with it.

About how much money does it cost to open a brewery?

I started my brewery with about $25,000. If I had to pay for equipment (7bbl minimum), a space, and hire folks, it would cost about $1M here in Portland...

In the past few years we have seen a massive surge in the popularity of Hazy IPA's and Sours, what do you believe the next popular beer style will be?

I think lagers, pilsners and kölsch are going to see a resurgence. The lesson with hard seltzer is people are wanting lower calories and less alcohol. Perhaps, hopefully, they'll start wanting flavor again.

When you first opened the brewery, what was the biggest obstacle? What advice would you give someone thinking about opening a brewery to avoid some of the pitfalls you experienced?

Getting started with anything new is tough. You will never know everything and someone will always be better than you at something. The best advice I could give is, ask for help. Don't be afraid of the unknown and learn to run a business. Have a plan and stick to it. It is a lot cheaper to make mistakes on paper before laying out a ton of cash and then finding out your plan isn't profitable.

What sets your brewery apart from most others?

We are going for story. I think many breweries can produce a quality product, but their stories aren't cohesive or compelling. Our branding gets people interested in who we are, then the great beer brings them back. Every beer gets a story to temp our customers to give us a try.

How do you decide on new beers to brew?

We brew what we like. Then listen to the customer. If they like one of our beers more, we'll brew it more often. We try to offer a little bit of everything so no one is left out.

How did you first discover craft beer and what made you want to enter the business?

I was working in the Information Technology field for many years. I loved craft beer and thought it would be fun to try my hand at making it. Once I did, I found that I loved every aspect of it. The science, the people, the craft, the creativity, the history... these are all things that made me fall in love with it and want to open my own.

End of a long brew day, what are you drinking?

It depends. I often find myself grabbing a traditional IPA, but will also grab a kölsch or stout.

What are a few beers that other brewers are making that you really find impressive?

Sours. I haven't really gotten into them as a brewer. I find that I cannot drink much of them as they don't react well to my insides, but the flavors are amazing.

How do you feel the internet has changed the way the craft brewing industry operates?

Without the internet, a small business like mine would not even get started. I can do much of the work of sales & marketing online for a lot less than hiring professionals. (for now) I can sell directly to customers without a physical location.

Does glassware really make a difference?

For sure! Proper glassware provides a vehicle for the beverage that accentuates the style and unique character of a beer. I hate drinking out of cans and bottles now. I want to be able to see the clarity, the effervescence, the color. I want the aroma to be properly delivered to my nostrils. I want the flavor to be preserved and unadulterated by dirt or rusty cap or whatever else might be on the container. Proper, clean, glassware does this.

What's the real difference between a Porter and a Stout?

This is a touchy topic nowadays, but if you look at the history of the terms, you'll find that the term "Stout" referred to the strength of a beer in percent alcohol by volume whereas "Porter" referred to the style (a dark beer, popular with river porters in London). So, you could have a stout amber, stout blonde, or stout porter. Today, people typically think of "Stout" as the dark style of beer and "Porter" is a dryer/roastier version that is often lighter in color, more brown than black.

How important is IBU when it comes to picking out a beer? Do customers need to pay attention to it?

This is personal choice. It can be misleading however. If a beer is well balanced, the IBU is meaningless. I think it can be helpful for beers that are hop-forward vs malt or yeast-forward. If a customer doesn't like über bitter beers, this can be helpful in steering them away from them. Most of the time, it's just interesting info that some people like to geek out on.

LAZY BOY BREWING

715 100th St SE Ste A1
Everett, WA 98208

Shawn Loring

Typically, how much beer do you guys make in a year?

We typically produce 1500-1800 bbls per year.

How much beer do you personally consume on an average workday?

I typically drink 1-2 craft beers daily

What's the style most fun to brew?

The most fun style to make for me right now is the Hazy IPA

What are the biggest obstacles to continued craft beer growth?

The biggest challenge is distribution

When you first opened the brewery, what was the biggest obstacle? What advice would you give someone thinking about opening a brewery to avoid some of the pitfalls you experienced?

One the things that people fail to think about when they open is the amount of feet on the streets to keep your business moving forward.

LOCUST LANE CRAFT BREWERY

50 Three Tun Rd Ste 4
Malvern, PA 19355

Tom

Typically, how much beer do you guys produce in an average year?

500 to 100 Barrels and growing

How much beer do you personally consume on an average workday?

None to one maybe after the day is over. Drinking while working with boiler wort is not a good idea.

What's your favorite food to eat with beer and why?

A nice burger. What's better than a beer and burger?

About how much money does it cost to open a brewery?

Min $500k but the sky is the limit. It depends on what size brewery you want to start out as and what equipment you want to buy.

What are today's worst beer trends?

Interesting question. I think the haphazard rating sites are an issue. They are a great place to find beers and keep track of beers that someone has had but the ratings are awful. It's not standardized at all so someone can say beer is awesome and give it a 3 and another can say the same but give it a 5. Also customers aren't educated on rating the beer based on the style. They can give a 1 when they just don't like that style even if the beer is good for that style.

In the past few years we have seen a massive surge in the popularity of Hazy IPA's and Sours, what do you believe the next popular beer style will be?

No idea. I wish I knew. Maybe brut IPAs but who knows. Low calorie, low carb beers are making a bit run now.

When you first opened the brewery, what was the biggest obstacle? What advice would you give someone thinking about opening a brewery to avoid some of the pitfalls you experienced?

My advice would be to be sure you know your costs. Costs of ingredients. Costs to can. Costs of labor. Etc. All anyone sees is what they paid for a beer but that's just a small part of the story.

What beers are you best known for and why?

I'm not completely sure. We get a lot of complements on our Kolsch, Amber Lager and lighter beers. We also sell a lot of IPAs so who's to tell. I hope we known as well rounded.

What sets your brewery apart from most others?

Maybe being a brewery that makes every style, not just IPA or Belgians or whatever. We want to give the customer a mix to choose from.

What are the biggest reasons for the continual growth of craft breweries?

First, it won't last forever. Right now we are stealing customers from the big guys like Inbev, Coors, etc. Smaller guys like us are also stealing some from the larger craft. Luckily there's a lot of money to go around.

How do you reach beyond the hardcore beer drinkers and into the general public to sell your beer?

A lot as we want to be the brewery that makes something for everyone. The hardcore beer drinkers are actually a small piece of the market.

How did you first discover craft beer and what made you want to enter the business?

We drank a lot Yuengling back in the day and we also went to Victory when it first opened. We got into this just by having fun making beer at home and thinking we could do something we like for a living. It's that simple.

What's the style most fun to brew?

Honestly, the easy ones are the most fun for me. Kolsch for example is easy and fun.

Is there a popular beer you make that you just don't really like but everyone else loves?

We have a beer called Sugartown Simcoe IPA that does really well. I don't like Simcoe by itself so it's not may favorite.

End of a long brew day, what are you drinking?

Water. It's hot brewing, especially in summer.

When coming out with a new brew, how much experimentation do you try to get in before you say it's ready for production?

Really very little. We are small enough that we can just go for it. If it doesn't work, it's not the end of the world.

What style of beer is your bestseller and why do you think that is?

Style would be IPA because... IPA.

What's the real difference between a Porter and a Stout?

Stout has more roasted malts than a porter. Porters a bit lighter in color and dark malt flavor than a stout. At least they should be.

How important is IBU when it comes to picking out a beer? Do customers need to pay attention to it?

IBU should not matter at all. IBU is a personally perceived thing. So 50 IBU to me would mean something different than 50 IBU to you. I would not recommend someone paying attention to it. We don't show it on our menu for example.

LOST WORLDS BREWING COMPANY

19700-D One Norman Way
Cornelius, NC 28031

Dave Hamme
Innovation & Operations

Writers Note:
This is a brand new brewery only open for a few months

Typically, how much beer do you guys make in a year?

We plan on 600 barrels this year (2020)

How much beer do you personally consume on an average workday?

One to two beers

What's your favorite food to eat with beer and why?

Sandwiches - it helps absorb the beer

About how much does it cost to open a brewery?

Depends to a large extent on the facility and how much work has to be done. I'd say it averages 1-2 million - although that number is going up.

What are today's worst beer trends?

I'm not a fan of breweries making seltzers - I hope that is just a fad. I'm also not a fan of the "Hop" bomb IPAs that seem to be so prevalent. I like a clean, well brewed IPA.

When you first opened the brewery, what was the biggest obstacle? What advice would you give someone thinking about opening a brewery to avoid some pitfalls you experienced?

The Pandemic hit us full force. I think the key is to be nimble. Take time to understand the trends and make adjustments to your business model. We pivoted to canning beers and we are now in roughly a dozen locations.

How do you decide on new beers to brew?

Market research and more market research. We wanted to know everything about the surrounding community and ensure we crafted brews that fit our audiences lifestyle.

How did you first discover craft beer and what made you want to enter the business?

I've been a homebrewer for years. I loved the unique flavors and styles that craft breweries were making. End of day, I got into the industry because I saw it as a great business opportunity and it would be a lot of fun.

What beer would you brew if cost, production, and sales were no object?

A Rauch Beer. While there is minimal market for it - a well brewed Rauch beer is one of the best styles out there.

Does glassware really make a difference?

Depends - we have our logo on our glasses and think of it as a marketing expense. Everyone cautioned against it. As to mixing glassware styles with beers, we do it on a limited basis. Folks have gotten used to drinking IPA's out of pint glasses so any special glassware is an unnecessary expense.

What beer is your brewery best known for and why?

Vista (West Coast IPA) and Euchre (Golden Ale). These are our two canned beers and they are picking up a loyal following. Craft breweries just don't brew these beers in the same way we do. They are clean, refreshing, and simple.

End of a long brew day, what are you drinking?

Vista IPA - just a smooth IPA with a ton of flavor.

LAND-GRANT BREWING COMPANY

424 W Town St
Columbus, OH 43215

CHRIS HELDERMAN
BREWERY PRODUCTION MANAGER

Typically, how much beer do you guys make in a year?

10,000 bbls

How much beer do you personally consume on an average workday?

It depends on the day but 2-4 is normal.

What's your favorite food to eat with beer and why?

My favorite food is definitely pizza (all flavors and kinds) and beer and
pizza happen to go fantastic together. The variety of flavor combos are

enormous, from a crisp Pilsner with Pepperoni and Banana Peppers, to fruity NEPA with a deep dish.

What are today's worst beer trends?

I really don't dislike any of the trends but I don't like taking shortcuts to get flavors or appearances that are very achievable using knowledge and quality ingredients.

How do you decide on new beers to brew?

This process varies. Sometimes brewers come up with amazing ideas that go up the flagpole and they are a hit. Other times Sales/Marketing comes up with an idea and the brewers get to work on executing the plan.

How did you first discover craft beer and what made you want to enter the business?

I started homebrewing in college and loved the science and process of brewing. Once you meet people in the industry you find it is a very large awesome community of breweries and people that just want to make better beer and have the craft industry grow. It is extremely collaborative and you don't find that in many industries.

What beer would you brew if cost, production, and sales were no object?

Malt forward beers in general do not sell as well as IPAs, or fruit beers, or anything else really. There is so much you can do with malt and some awesome craft maltsters out there that are coming up with new stuff all the time that the possibilities are exciting. I have always been a fan of Best Bitters. Awesome malt flavor, sessionable, and goes great with or without food.

Does glassware really make a difference?

Short answer is, YES! When are trying to pick up all the flavors and aromas there can be a huge difference between a shaker pint and the appropriate glassware. We can our beers so I usually drink my beers out of cans, but when trying a new beer or relaxing I try to use appropriate glassware.

What beer is your brewery best known for and why?

Either Stiff-Arm IPA which was one of our first beers brewed and the first craft beer in Ohio Stadium or Pool Party Pilsner which is a summer seasonal New Zealand Style Pilsner that is our most refreshing beer.

End of a long brew day, what are you drinking?

I usually go for either end of the spectrum, either a crisp lager or an extremely hoppy DIPA.

LOCHIEL BREWING

7143 E Southern Ave Ste 131
Mesa, AZ 85209

Ian Cameron
Owner

Typically, how much beer do you guys make in a year?

1500 barrels

How much beer do you personally consume on an average workday?

2-3 pints

What's your favorite food to eat with beer and why?

Pizza, because I can drink a variety of beers with it.

About how much does it cost to open a brewery?

Way too much, but in the range of 500k to 750k for a 10bbl brewery.

What are today's worst beer trends?

Same old boring IPA, being passed off as something new!

When you first opened the brewery, what was the biggest obstacle? What advice would you give someone thinking about opening a brewery to avoid some pitfalls you experienced?

Licensing, finding common grounds between Federal, State, County, and Municipal laws and codes and finding a location that is accepting of a brewery.

How do you decide on new beers to brew?

Family recipes handed down from generations of family brewers.

How did you first discover craft beer and what made you want to enter the business?

Exposure from a previous generation family brewer showing the ropes at the young age of 10 and on.

What beer would you brew if cost, production, and sales were no object?

Jacobite Scotch Heavy Ale (14% ABV)

Does glassware really make a difference?

Yes. How the beer is aerated, delivered, and opened up as the pour down the throat goes.

What beer is your brewery best known for and why?

Scotch Wee Heavy Ale and the Jacobite Scotch Heavy Ale

End of a long brew day, what are you drinking?

Fusilier Scottish Lager (Pale lager type) 4.5% ABV.

LONG BREWING

29380 NE Owls Ln
Newberg, OR 97132

Paul Long

Writers Note
Paul was kind enough to give a detailed explanation about his brewery so I
will include it in it's entirety.

We are a very small brewery in the middle of Oregon wine country. What
sets us apart is our "No Compromise" approach. Our tag line is "Fine
Ales and Lagers". A significant part of our market is wineries and wine
drinkers who value fine beers. We have the luxury of using the best of
everything to produce clean, well balanced beers with aroma and flavors
that can rival that of wines. We use ALL whole hops. Our IPA is still the
most popular with hops sourced right from the drying pile at the growers
and vacuum packed and frozen. We even get the same variety hop from

multiple fields finding that they are VERY different. We then choose the best fields to layer and balance our IPA. We also use the "right" yeast for every beer style because yeast really defines the beer. At the end of a day I usually go for a nice Kolsch, our second most popular beer.

LOOKOUT BREWING COMPANY

103 S Ridgeway Ave
Black Mountain, NC 28711

John Garcia
"Brewgineer"

Typically, how much beer do you guys produce in an average year?

We have been making about 250-300 BBL's of beer per year for the past few years. We sell all of it in house. We have done some minor distribution, but have not done so for the past year and a half due to our growing demand in house.

How much beer do you personally consume on an average workday?

On an average day, I usually consume about 2 pints of beer.

What's your favorite food to eat with beer and why?

My favorite food to eat with beer is Mexican food. I like the social aspect of drinking and Mexican food meals usually tend to be communal meals. I like to eat and drink with people.

About how much money does it cost to open a brewery?

The amount of money needed to start a brewery is.....more. You will always need more. I am different than most breweries in that I am able to do most of the work needed to open and run a brewery on my own. I installed the glycol, floor drains, electrical, construction, plumbing, draft lines, wood work, on and on. I have some amazing friends and family members that are always down to lend a hand and we just get it done. My amount of money needed to open might have been lower than most, but the answer will always be MORE.

What are today's worst beer trends?

I think today's worst trend in beer is politics. I feel that this industry is best served by the creativity and collaboration of ideas and styles and general artisanship. The interference of big business and politics tends to restrict that atmosphere. When people get into this industry and don't have a passion for it, the industry suffers. It has been apparent on a large scale over the past 3-4 years in particular with the large acquisitions and distribution stronghold enforcement in certain states.

In the past few years we have seen a massive surge in the popularity of Hazy IPA's and Sours, what do you believe the next popular beer style will be?

I think the next big trend in beers will be light beer. Lagers are the number one seller in the world so it's hard to say it will be the next trend, but craft lagers are amazing and better than the big brand lagers. I think that will be a focus for our brewery. Hazy IPA's will probably take over as the biggest single craft style. Once people begin to taste what a great NEIPA can be, they will demand more. Right now, there are just a lot of not very good examples and it's still growing faster than anything else on the market.

When you first opened the brewery, what was the biggest obstacle? What advice would you give someone thinking about opening a brewery to avoid some of the pitfalls you experienced?

The largest obstacle in opening the brewery would be the operational aspect. Getting the books in order, getting licensing, submitting label applications, reporting all the numbers, and just the general daily office work would be the most difficult part. If you are gonna have partners, don't get another brewer, get an amazing office asset. That is one of the main differences between good breweries and great ones.

What beers are you best known for and why?

We are best known for our Mountain Hopshine. It outsells all of our other beers by a good bit. It is a NEIPA that uses Citra hops. It is simply delicious. We make it a little more bitter than a lot of NEIPA's. That is a personal preference. We make a lot of NEIPA's and we will be putting out some in the very near future that will probably be better, but the OG will probably have staying power. When I stray to other beers and I don't have one for a while, it always surprises me when I get back to it and I often ask myself why I stayed away for so long. It is great.

What sets your brewery apart from most others?

There are a lot of things that set us apart from other breweries. I would start with our team. We have an awesome team that is very close and we all have big roles in what our little brewery does. Our bartenders have just as much say in what we brew as the brewer does. We meet all the time and bounce ideas around. It is what makes this place go. I would also add that we are very comfortable with making our product. We feel that our beer is just better than it's ever been before due to our comfort in how we brew and how we decide what to brew next. We generally know when we are making something that will be delicious.

How do you decide on new beers to brew?

We talk a lot about beer. I usually have some crazy idea and then we all talk about it for a few meetings and make it. The Gose has been lingering longer than usual, but it will happen this summer. Usually the process is fairly quick. Our GM also brings in a lot of new ideas for the next beer. She has some great ideas and between her and the main brewer, they usually bring some pretty polished ideas to the table. We also drink together a lot and that breeds some good creativity.

What are the biggest reasons for the continual growth of craft breweries?

The continual growth of breweries is most likely due to the atmosphere that most of them create. When you have creative people doing things around a highly social beverage, good things happen. Walking into our tasting room gives people a sense of community and comfort. We hear people say things like "it feels like I'm at a friend's house" or "this feels like a living room" quite often. People like the ambiance of a place that only offers a "want" vs. a "need".

What are the biggest obstacles to continued craft beer growth?

For my brewery in particular, the biggest obstacle would be securing financing. That is probably different than the industry as a whole though. I do things quite differently and banks usually don't like that. I own almost everything in the building and don't carry a debt load. Therefor, my credit doesn't match my assets. It's hard to get loans to grow. As an industry as a whole, I'd say politics get in the way most of the time. All the red tape and bullshit of taxes and paperwork are big hurdles.

What are the biggest problems you run into in producing beer?

The biggest problems that I run into in producing beer would usually be storage and supply. Managing all of our ingredients and having them there on time to brew is a little bit of a juggling act. Having enough storage to keep things available, especially cold storage, is sometimes a logjam.

How do you reach beyond the hardcore beer drinkers and into the general public to sell your beer?

We reach our audience mainly through community activism and community building events. We reach the general beer drinkers though hosting events, supporting events, sponsoring community needs/programs and generally being active in our community. We also typically have a light beer on tap for the newer craft drinker. Experienced and hardcore craft enthusiasts also enjoy our lighter offerings. I find myself drinking a lot of lager when I'm out simply due to the refreshing quality and the lower abv.

How did you first discover craft beer and what made you want to enter the business?

I first discovered craft beer at Dr. Rockets in Corpus Christi Texas. Fat Tire was just starting to sell beer in Texas and they were having a release party at Dr. Rockets. One of my friends was playing music that night and we had Fat Tire all evening. It was good and tasted totally different than all the regular beer I was used to. It was more palatable than the pale ales and other craft offering. Easy to drink and just downright good. I then started to try more varieties over the coming months until I developed a taste for hops thank to Sierra Nevada Pale Ale. I began brewing and started a brewery for a lot of reasons that would take up a longer email than this current one.

How do you attempt to increase beer production while still staying true to both your brand and your unique styles?

We will attempt to increase our production and create better consistency by growing to a larger system. I will not be changing our core values by growing. We are also not looking to grow to compete on a macro level or anything. We simply want to grow naturally as opportunities come to us.

What's the style most fun to brew?

The most fun styles to brew for me personally are the dark beers. While I drink IPA's and lagers more often than stouts, the stouts certainly feel the most fun to brew. The whole brewhouse and taproom has this amazing smell and the malts make me think of being snowed in at a Vermont cabin in the woods. It reminds me of sitting by a huge hearth with friends and family. They are easily my favorite thing to brew.

What beer would you brew if cost, production, and sales were no object?

When all things are set aside and I just brew what I want to brew, I would make NEIPA's. They are simply the best beers I have ever had. If I could only choose one, it would be pretty easy to choose that. Ultimately I would want a large variety of options, but I could live with just a big juice bomb.

Is there a popular beer you make that you just don't really like but everyone else loves?

There are a couple of our beers that I wouldn't want to drink all of the time, but I don't dislike any of them. Dark beers in general aren't my cup of tea (or beer) but I enjoy them in the right setting and sparingly.

End of a long brew day, what are you drinking?

At the end of a hard day of brewing, I am drinking our Watershed Lager. It is just too easy to drink, light bodied, and low alcohol which are traits I usually want after hard work. I sometimes opt for the Hopshine but with a 7% abv, I can only have a few.

What are a few beers that other brewers are making that you really find impressive?

I am still wowed every time I have a Pliny. I don't like that it is hard to get and has all the hype, but in the same breath, it is worth it. It was the first mega star that I had and it fulfilled expectations. I remember my first one. We were having a beer tasting party and by the end of that pint, I said "I get it". Everybody else agreed, it's just really good. Treehouse would be my crush though. I absolutely love their IPA's. They are great. Trillium's beautiful labels as well as their really good beer are also up there. Sip of Sunshine changed my world and made me dive headfirst in to brewing NEIPA's. It's super good too.

How do you feel the internet has changed the way the craft brewing industry operates?

The internet has simply changed the availability of sharing ideas so well that I feel like we can confidently teach and learn in real time. If I want to learn about a style of a specific beer, I can get the information I need in a few seconds. It also allows for different kinds of advertising. The social media reach is so powerful and helps us share with others so broadly that I cannot imagine being without. It certainly has it's negatives as well, by it is a strong tool more often than not.

When coming out with a new brew, how much experimentation do you try to get in before you say it's ready for production?

We will usually brew a test batch a few times as a 3 barrel experiment before making 12 or 15 barrels. There are a few that go in immediately to production. Our latest stout, west coast IPA, and NEIPA only got 1 test batch and we're already putting them into the big tanks.

What style of beer is your best seller and why do you think that is?

The New England IPA is our best selling style. It is easy for new craft drinkers to enjoy because it is not harsh or bitter. It is easy for experienced and seasoned craft drinkers to enjoy because of it's complex hop aromas and subtle malt variations. It is easy for wine drinkers to enjoy because of the fruit aspects of the aromas. It is simply and amazing style when done well.

Does glassware really make a difference?

Glassware does make a difference. People drink and eat with their eyes. When we switched to a much nicer glass with nucleation on the bottom and a nicer logo done in gold, it changed out drinker's perception of what they were consuming. We have a lot of people that comment of our glassware and we even have some theft of it. While theft is not good for us, I figure that person will truly enjoy that glass and they really wanted it. We sell them as well, but I'd guess that those stolen glasses will probably have a few extra stories around them and will probably be remembered by that customer with some fond memories. In the future, I would like to offer a better variety of glass ware so that we could offer a pilsner glass and a stout goblet and so forth. It gives the consumer an instant reminder that we probably know what we're doing if they get a specific glass for their specific beer.

What's the real difference between a Porter and a Stout?

The porter and the stout....the real difference is in the spelling. As for the way I brew them, I go for a heavier body on the stout. I mash it at a different temperature. I have longer sugar chains in the stout giving it a higher finishing gravity. I typically try to give it a darker foam and more specialty malts. I try to make porters more like a dark version of an ale. It is brewed at a standard temperature and I usually use the same percentage of specialty malts as I would in a regular ale. It just happens to have bigger and darker specialty malts. I think with the new brew system we are hoping to upgrade to in the near future, we'll be able to do more with these styles and play with different temperature rests and really get to making some super cool malt profiles.

How important is IBU when it comes to picking out a beer? Do customers need to pay attention to it?

IBU's are certainly important for people that know what they want out of a beer. Bitterness is not for everyone. If you have a really high abv, you should probably look for high IBU as well. At least I do. I don't like that sweetness that comes with 8.5% abv. I also like higher IBU's in my west coast IPA's. The more informed you are, the more focused your decision can be. But at the same time, people who choose between vanilla and chocolate tend to be happier with their decision after they have their ice cream. Strange how that works, huh?

LIONHEART PUB AND BREWERY

448 Madison Ave #3601,
Albany, NY 12208

John Kivelin
Brewer

From the brewer: We were a relatively popular bar in Albany, NY that catered to regulars in midtown Albany during happy hours and a younger college student crowd in the evenings. We started in 1992 as one of the area's first craft beer bars. We found it difficult to fill the 16 taps with unique beers. We moved to a larger building in 2003 and had 36 craft beers on tap. Last year we doubled our space by expanding to our second floor and adding a small two-barrel system to brew beers for in house consumption only. Now we have 45 craft beers on tap only three of which are ours. We use the brewery to enhance the charm and increase the patronage of an already popular bar. We have three unique beers on tap at any time. The brewery is basically an advanced home brew setup. In fact, my equipment is basically scaled up versions of what I learned to brew on.

Braumeister 50 Liter is now a Braumeister 200 L system. Same with the conical fermenters (62 L) and the 1 bbl brite tanks (I use two per batch). Something that makes us different due to our business model is that I can have fun with my ingredients because I'm never trying to shave a few cents off the price since we are already. Bottom line is that when you sell a beer for $6 that has $0.40-$0.60 in ingredients, shaving a few cents off the cost is largely irrelevant. Obviously, this business model would be catastrophic for a brewery that was also bottling, distributing, paying wholesalers, retailers, while also trying to sell 12 oz for $2.00-$2.25. Probably, the most unique thing we do with the brewery (since ingredient cost isn't really a huge factor) is we use reverse osmosis systems to purify all water and then build the water profile to the region of the beer's origin for any beer that has a honed in origin story. I use Guinness Wicklow Mtn for stouts, London and Dublin water profiles for different porters, specific German water profiles for German beer, and the same goes for Belgium. Using reverse osmosis and salts to attain the exact water profile is much more costly than just treating the water to get it close enough. The same goes for our yeast. We try our best to attain the regional liquid yeast or use Imperial liquid yeast to try to match the original beer style as closely as possible instead of using Salafe-04 or Salafe-05 like many small to midsize breweries use. I'm not sure how much these things actually affect the flavor to the average beer drinker, but it makes me feel like I have tried to make something as close to historically accurate as possible.

Typically, how much beer do you guys produce in an average year?

We produce approximately 2,600 gallons of beer per year for consumption on site only.

How much beer do you personally consume on an average workday?

Probably 3-4 beers 3-4 times per week. I also began intermittently fast for periods of 3-14 days at a time during the previous few months. These fasts are incredible at helping to reset the body using a process called autophagy that causes the body to consume damaged cells, which theoretically helps shrink the liver. So, I probably don't drink or eat at all for usually one, maybe even two weeks of the month, but when I do - as stated above - probably 3-4 beers 3-4 times per week.

What's your favorite food to eat with beer and why?

Man, I love almost any food with beer! We serve large 10" soft pretzels and flatbread pizzas, which are great, but I really love eating chicken wings from local businesses with beer. Something about trying to wash away the hot sauce and never quite getting the gratification.

About how much money does it cost to open a brewery?

This is kind of a two-part question. Our equipment cost just under $80,000, but most of the actual large costs from the serving space is already spent keeping the bar open. However, that cost would be insane compared to what we spent if you included the bottling line, warehouse, and all of the staff and other stuff required to sell off-site. As I stated above, a brew pub that serves on site only is almost a different business altogether when compared to a commercial brewery designed for purely off-site consumption.

What are today's worst beer trends?

My least favorite trend is less about an actual beer, and more about the drinking trends. It seems like patrons are always looking for the next big thing or niche brand. This makes it nearly impossible for a small region brewery to stay afloat when they are mostly trying to distribute off-site. A brewery that is both learning and growing struggles to keep the doors open. Just when they get things right and find their strides, two or three small breweries open that make average – or even below average beer. The original brewery loses market share that they desperately fought and grew for, ultimately struggling to pay the bills. Many end up going under and selling their equipment, and even spaces, for pennies on the dollar to a third generation of young energetic entrepreneurs who are next in line to put the 2nd generation of breweries out of business. None of this really affects my brew pub since we make our money selling beers from all of those reference generations. We don't really care if you drink our beer, as long as you love the beer in your hand.

In the past few years we have seen a massive surge in the popularity of Hazy IPA's and Sours, what do you believe the next popular beer style will be?

I think it will be the Kolsch style. The Kolsch style is a great "gateway" beer that can get people who usually only drink light American lagers to begin to enjoy more robust craft beers. It would be in the craft beer industry's best interest to develop this style or others like it, which will draw Americans toward the beer that they deserve. I tell people all of the time that light American lagers developed the best marketing scheme of all time. They convinced the blue collar American that light beer that is the least expensive to make, and generally has no real flavor or body to note is "what real men drink" while they convinced the same vast majority of Americans that flavorful robust beers with expensive ingredient lists are for snobs. Next, they will convince the same American's that steak is for snobs and that tofu is what real men eat. I am not even mad about it. I am sincerely amazed at what happened to beer in the 40's-50's based on a nothing short of incredible marketing scheme.

When you first opened the brewery, what was the biggest obstacle? What advice would you give someone thinking about opening a brewery to avoid some of the pitfalls you experienced?

I can honestly say that I really did not have any big obstacles. The renovation was funded by the owner who had an epic vision and invested in himself. However, from listening to some other owners, I'd say that the three obstacles you need to figure out before trying to do this is: 1) Have a buy-out plan with any partner including family and friends... especially family and friends! One person always thinks they did more work, while others feel that they were the brains/visionary, while even others believe that they invested while the business was on the ground floor and are just along for the ride, reaping the financial benefits. There needs to be a well thought out, written plan that lays this all out while partners are both civil and friends. 2) Control growth, always staying a little bit lean in supply letting demand stay just above supply at the expense of losing some profits. Responsible growth has destroyed many breweries that overgrew supply with regional demand and could not afford to pay the bills. 3) Figure out how to get funding without creating indefinite partnerships that will destroy profits as the brewery grows. I.e. Have a buy out plan for investors as well.

What beers are you best known for and why?

We swap our beer styles all of the time, so we are not known for just one. I guess it would compare more to a small restaurant with a menu that only consists of specials that change every week.

What sets your brewery apart from most others?

As stated above, it is the fact that we are a popular bar with a brewery that enhances it. This allows us to have fun making different beers for people to try – along with the other 45 craft beers on tap. Again, we don't care if you are drinking our beer, as long as you love what you are drinking, where you are sitting, and are enjoying time with friends.

How do you decide on new beers to brew?

We look at the different styles diagrams/bubble charts and try to explore styles we haven't brewed before. We do have a few that are IPA or extra pale ales which people love, so we repeat those periodically as well. Obviously, season plays a large role in how we choose beer styles as well with lighter styles being served during warmer periods.

What are the biggest reasons for the continual growth of craft breweries?

Unfortunately, I think it is because people are always looking for the next new thing or new brand. This has been catastrophic for a lot of brewers.

What are the biggest obstacles to continued craft beer growth?

As discussed above, I think it will be the constant desire for new brands combined with a shortage of "gateway" beers being created and sold by the industry that can draw the lion's share of drinkers from light American lagers.

What are the biggest problems you run into in producing beer?

The biggest problem has been the COVID virus, which has created uncertainty in the bar and restaurant industry. Several batches of beer that were made in the week or two prior to the shutdown, which are probably on their last leg. Moreover, it is nearly impossible to know when/if to begin the next batch based on total fact-free speculation about what the states will do. I was 100% confident that states could not afford to shut down for 90+ days, yet here we are.

How do you reach beyond the hardcore beer drinkers and into the general public to sell your beer?

We really don't try to alter spending habits to sell our beer. "Drink the beer you are comfortable with, if we don't make it, we definitely sell it anyway."

How did you first discover craft beer and what made you want to enter the business?

My uncle began the business as a craft beer bar in 1992. I spent 23 years in the Marine Corps, where I served as an infantry officer. I had a degree in Mechanical Engineering and loved brewing beer. The degree helped me get things in the brewery setup since engineering is basically professional problem solving and setting up/running a brewery is basically problem solving. My service helped to put things in perspective. Basically, every day is pretty easy and a blast compared to the rigors of day-to-day service in the Marine Corps. The service also taught me to laugh all the time and have fun, especially when things are not funny and not fun. Essentially, I go to work every day to do my hobby, with my favorite person (my uncle is incredibly funny), at the one place I dreamt of coming back to when I was away from home during my time in the service. (Literally, whenever I dreamed at night that I was back home in Albany, it was always at some weird dream version of my uncle's bar.)

How do you attempt to increase beer production while still staying true to both your brand and your unique styles?

Fortunately, we don't really have to choose to compromise between beer production and staying true to the brand/unique styles. We have an excess capacity to brew probably 100% more than we could possibly need.

What's the style most fun to brew?

I love dark beers! The smell is great when brewing, and they are the most fun to taste and drink with friends since there is so much flavor in them. IPAs and NEIPAs can be stressful since everyone has an opinion (all valid), but I cannot tell you how many times within 5 minutes, I'll have a customer give me a bland review of my beer. "It's good, but a bit too light on x, y, or z" while a second patron will approach me and tell me that "It is incredible. Do not change a thing!" Turns out brewing, like pizza and sex, is pretty easy. Put great ingredients into the equipment at the correct times and temperatures with a solid process, and you are going to get pretty good beer. Some people will love it, and others will not. There is no magic elf urinating on the back of a unicorn that I have to catch just perfectly into the brite tank to make great beer (although some brewers would want you to believe that).

What beer would you brew if cost, production, and sales were no object?

I already brew whatever beer we want since cost and sales is no object? Even if we could drive the cost of a batch up to $1.50 in ingredients per 12 oz, we still have no cost associated with bottling, wholesaler cut, retailer cut, distribution costs, no costs associated with losses in these processes. Our beer goes from mash tun, to a fermenter 6' away. From there it is wheeled ~6' into the warming room to rest, before it is wheeled ~6' away to the cooler to be cold crashed and pumped into the brite tanks (~4' away). The brite tanks connect straight to the upstairs and downstairs taps. The three beers that we serve on tap reside in tanks that are within 36 inches from the mash tun where they were brewed.

Is there a popular beer you make that you just don't really like but everyone else loves?

Not really, but I do have the opposite problem. I love Irish Red Ales and Belgian Dubbels. They came out excellent, but will never sell nearly as an average IPA.

End of a long brew day, what are you drinking?

If it is dart league night, I am drinking a dark porter/stout. Most other times, probably an IPA/NEIPA.

What are a few beers that other brewers are making that you really find impressive?

NEIPAs are something that have been hit or miss for me. They really break all of the rules of the traditional brewing process. Many, if not most, don't use any hops in the boil which theoretically, should give them almost zero bitterness since it is almost 100% oils in no real resin. The murkiness is also something I struggle with since I set up the brewery to clarify as much as possible. Even the murkiest NEIPA I make struggles to stay cloudy when sitting at 31 degrees cold crashing for a week, followed by a few weeks in the brewery brite tanks which are also held at 31 degrees. Sloop Juice, Juice Bomb and Fiddlehead are some of the best beers I have had. Additionally, Frog Alley Brewing produces consistently excellent beers that are well balanced and taste exactly true to style every time I've tasted one.

How do you feel the internet has changed the way the craft brewing industry operates?

Obviously, Beermenus and Untappd have helped the industry tremendously, but I would say that Instagram has done more for NEIPAs than any other aspect of the internet. The style is so unbelievably photogenic, and every post makes me want to drink something juicy, even though much of the time, I prefer traditional IPAs to the dankness of many NEIPAs.

When coming out with a new brew, how much experimentation do you try to get in before you say it's ready for production?

Most of the stuff I have brewed at home in the previous years, but our operation is so small and all of the beers rotate often. We do not do much experimentation at all for that reason, although I am always trying to tweak my brewing process to produce beers with no off flavors. Remember that our setup is as small or smaller than most commercial brewery pilot systems.

What style of beer is your bestseller and why do you think that is?

As I mentioned above, any pale ale, IPA or NEIPA sell pretty fast. It just seems to be what people want from their beer at the present moment. I can't say I blame them. They are great, refreshing beers.

Does glassware really make a difference?

I believe that it does. Drinking beer is so much more than just the flavor. It is the experience. It is the people around you. It is the time of day. It is the smell of the room, and the humidity in the air, as well as the temperature and breeze. If I tell someone what they are about to taste, they get excited every time even if they don't love the style. If I make them guess, they get suspicious of the beer and generally don't have as pleasant of an experience. The glassware is part of the experience that makes people feel that the experience is more special and – at a minimum - absolutely has a measurable placebo effect on the flavor, if nothing else.

What's the real difference between a Porter and a Stout?

If the books I read hold true, there is no difference except a one-word descriptor in the BJCP guidelines. I think "burnt" may be optional for Stouts. In reality, the two styles had deviated and mixed by different brewers in the United Kingdom/Ireland for approximately 100 years before someone tried to define each one as its own separate style. I think it was *Beer* by Charles Bamforth where he pointed this out and gave the example of the Guinness Stout (4.2%) ABV sitting on a store shelf next to an Imperial Baltic Porter (9.5% ABV). Consequently, the old adage "porters are lighter stouts" is out the window. However, just as I stated above, the descriptor has a placebo effect on the drinker. In my opinion, most people who have the preconceived notion that stouts are heavier and higher ABV will perceive those preconceived traits when they drink the beer based on the given style name. So as a brewer, what are you trying to market with the beer you are making. If you are going for a refreshing, but flavorful dark beer, that can be enjoyed all night, call it a porter. However, if you are trying to market a robust beer to drink with friends that will "get you to where you are going" in taking the edge off, call it a stout.

How important is IBU when it comes to picking out a beer? Do customers need to pay attention to it?

They should definitely pay attention to it if they are turned off by West Coast IPAs. I can't tell you how many times people have come into the bar and asked about different beers. When they are asked about IPAs, many reply, "Oh, I can't stand them! I don't know how people drink them!" Usually, this person was cruelly given something to the style effect of Stone Brewing Double Ruination Double IPA at 100+ IBUs. I believe most people can grow accustomed to IPAs and even double IPAs, but it is something that people need to be eased into. However, I don't think it is nearly as important if you are a customer who already enjoys extremely bitter beers. These customers can still enjoy pale ales and IPAs that hover on the cusp of 45 IBUs pretty easily.

LANCASTER BREWING CO.

302 N Plum St # 304
Lancaster, PA 17602

Peter Keares

Typically, how much beer do you guys make in a year?

In the neighborhood of 14,000 BBLs

How much beer do you personally consume on an average workday?

Not much during work

What's your favorite food to eat with beer and why?

It's hard to beat our half-pound cheeseburger or smoked brisket with a cold brew. Pizza always works too

About how much does it cost to open a brewery?

Far, far more than your initial budget regardless of brewery size. Unexpected circumstances are the norm

What are today's worst beer trends?

Macro brewing's invasion of craft, arrogant and condescending attitudes towards differing beer styles and breweries that brew ridiculously extreme beers just to gain attention

When you first opened the brewery, what was the biggest obstacle?

Cash flow

What advice would you give someone thinking about opening a brewery to avoid some pitfalls you experienced?

Be ready to work 20 hours a day, always estimate conservatively and have a solid plan but be prepared to change it along the way

How do you decide on new beers to brew?

Our Lancaster Jam Series of beers are where we have fun and at the same time research and develop new beers and techniques

How did you first discover craft beer and what made you want to enter the business?

Sam Adams and Pete's Wicked in the late 80's were game changers

What beer would you brew if cost, production, and sales were no object?

We don't cut any corners, so the same beer we brew now, although if we had more space, we'd likely barrel age a few more beers

Does glassware really make a difference?

Slightly but, more importantly, glassware needs to have a beer clean interior, free of any mineral deposits, debris, grease etc.

What beer is your brewery best known for and why?

We brew great German Lagers & IPAs, but are known for our stouts and pumpkin ale (Double Chocolate Milk Stout, Milk Stout, Baked Pumpkin Ale) Our Lancaster Milk Stout is America's original craft Milk Stout, brewed since 1994.

End of a long brew day, what are you drinking?

Usually a smooth, clean Lancaster Lager or low IBU, IPA like our Haze Farmer.

LENA BREWING COMPANY

9416 W Wagner Rd
Lena, IL 61048

Jaime Heddinger
Taproom Manager

Typically, how much beer do you guys produce in an average year?

20,000-25,000 gallons

How much beer do you personally consume on an average workday?

Depends on the day!! The brewers usually have a couple while work,
taking a break, after working.

What's your favorite food to eat with beer and why?

Anything, beer compliments all types of food. We actually host beer dinners

About how much money does it cost to open a brewery?

Way more than you really want to spend, you almost have to be mad at your money!

What are today's worst beer trends?

This is a forever changing business, I'm not sure there really are BAD beer trends. It is interesting to see the constant ebb and flow of styles of beers. When the craft beer scene REALLY hit, it was IPAs. Which scared people. I tell people all the time, drink what you like!

In the past few years we have seen a massive surge in the popularity of Hazy IPA's and Sours, what do you believe the next popular beer style will be?

This is SO true. It's hard to say, perhaps the next step is getting creative with unique and bizarre flavors.

When you first opened the brewery, what was the biggest obstacle? What advice would you give someone thinking about opening a brewery to avoid some of the pitfalls you experienced?

Consistency is KEY!!! and something we learned, from someone who learned the hard way, when you build, make sure you leave yourself with room to expand and grow. Don't try to go to big too fast, but set yourself up for success

What beers are you best known for and why?

We have some house and seasonal favorites. Our Drunkelberry, Black Rasp. Brown Wheat is a HUGE hit. In our rural Midwest area, people gravitate towards sweeter tastes. This beer has the same idea as a Radler, but with Black Rasp. instead of Grapefruit with a Dunkelweizen (Dark

Wheat) vs. a Hefeweizen (Light Wheat). But something we take pride in is offering a variety of styles. You can't pick just one favorite!

What sets your brewery apart from most others?

It's comfortable and friendly! The staff is knowledgeable and we focus on customer service! Besides the fact we have tasty beer, it's about the experience

How do you decide on new beers to brew?

We sit at a table and talk about the trends, keep up with our distributors, who know what people are looking for in the market, and pay attention to what people are asking for!

What are the biggest reasons for the continual growth of craft breweries?

People are starting to understand how good craft beer is!

What are the biggest obstacles to continued craft beer growth?

Something new and shiny coming along, however, I don't feel craft beer is going anywhere. It's a new understanding of beer that people are into

What are the biggest problems you run into in producing beer?

Back to consistency, making sure you product is the same EVERYTIME!

How do you reach beyond the hardcore beer drinkers and into the general public to sell your beer?

Tasting, tastings, tastings. We put ourselves out there as much as we can. We love a challenge and stand by our product! One way or another, we're going to win the hearts of those that "just don't drink beer"

How did you first discover craft beer and what made you want to enter the business?

Personally I've always been a bar girl and love trying things. Being in the business for over 20yrs you learn ALOT. However, the man that made it all happen, is a Midwest farm boy, who worked at his dads restaurant, then went on to work in Vegas a really discovered his love for craft beer and brought the idea back to good 'ol Lena

How do you attempt to increase beer production while still staying true to both your brand and your unique styles?

Stay tight and stay good! We try not to be the guy that has 4829330 different flavors. We make what we know is good and do that ... as much as we can and promote the ever living bageezy out of it!

What's the style most fun to brew?

We offer our "off the wall" taps. The experimental ones. I think the guys REALLY enjoy those. You get to play around!

What beer would you brew if cost, production, and sales were no object?

.... That's a tough one to answer

Is there a popular beer you make that you just don't really like but everyone else loves?

One of the brewers HATES coffee so our Caramel Pecan Coffee Stout, that is a house favorite, he wants NOTHING to do with!

End of a long brew day, what are you drinking?

The Haymow Molly Vienna Amber Lager. Easy and smooth

What are a few beers that other brewers are making that you really find impressive?

Imperials! They are a fine brew

How do you feel the internet has changed the way the craft brewing industry operates?

It's become a hipster life and thats ok!

When coming out with a new brew, how much experimentation do you try to get in before you say it's ready for production?

Depends on the brew! Sometimes, it's right on the money and sometimes it needs tweaking. However, it's not the cheapest to just experiment with beer, so one way or another we make something out of it!

What style of beer is your bestseller and why do you think that is?

Light and sweet! We are in the heart of Busch Light country, those are hards sells! :)

Does glassware really make a difference?

We believe so, just like wine, those nose is affected with the style glass. In Germany, this is a HUGE thing. You better be putting the right beer in the right glass!

What's the real difference between a Porter and a Stout?

Each is different, mostly roastiness!

How important is IBU when it comes to picking out a beer?

Do customers need to pay attention to it? Depends, in our area, people aren't even sure what IBU is, we teach them. But, unless they're a hop head, I think people are more concerned with ABV! That's how they shop.

MACKENZIE BREWING COMPANY

932 Meramec Station Road
Valley Park, MO 63088

Jeffrey Doss

Typically, how much beer do you guys produce in an average year?

We are very small – about 100 BBL per year

How much beer do you personally consume on an average workday?

1 – 12 or 16oz serving, our "shift beer"

What's your favorite food to eat with beer and why?

The pizza we make in house, when I eat.

About how much money does it cost to open a brewery?

That's a loaded question, depends on the condition of the building you're in, the size of your system, barrel aging storage if needed, etc. In general, I'd estimate a low average of $110K/BBL capacity

What are today's worst beer trends?

Low alcohol, N.A., SELTZER!!

When you first opened the brewery, what was the biggest obstacle? What advice would you give someone thinking about opening a brewery to avoid some of the pitfalls you experienced?

The biggest obstacle is probably recognition that you exist in your own neighborhood. Get very involved in the brewing community early (years) before opening.

What beers are you best known for and why?

We do Belgian-style Ales because that's what I love. Very small batches that take a long time to make right.

What sets your brewery apart from most others?

Oddly, we are very, very small and organized around a retail model instead of distribution – we distribute nothing.

How do you decide on new beers to brew?

Primarily seasons and how it aligns with the other beers we offer at the time. I hate a beer menu that starts with an IPA, ends with an IPA and are mostly IPA's in the middle.

What are the biggest problems you run into in producing beer?

Planning takes most of my time. I make only what we sell on site and have to time running out of a previous beer with the brewing/fermenting/aging of it's replacement so as not to have excessive stock un-necessarily aging or be out of a style for service.

How do you reach beyond the hardcore beer drinkers and into the general public to sell your beer?

Very slowly – not by choice. We donate a lot of gift cards and other brewery centric gifts to local schools and organizations for fund-raisers.

How do you attempt to increase beer production while still staying true to both your brand and your unique styles?

Sell more, Brew more. Marketing drives the whole equation.

What's the style most fun to brew?

We brew a Czech Pilsner and use a decoction brewing method. Long, hot and a giant mess; but you don't get the same taste otherwise-and it's a huge hit.

What beer would you brew if cost, production, and sales were no object?

Our same core Belgian-style Ales.

Is there a popular beer you make that you just don't really like but everyone else loves?

Cream Ale

End of a long brew day, what are you drinking?

Water

What are a few beers that other brewers are making that you really find impressive?

Locally, Modern Brewery's 'Citropolis IPA'. Not so locally, 3 Floyds 'Zombie versus Unicorn' and North Coast's 'Brother Thelonious'

When coming out with a new brew, how much experimentation do you try to get in before you say it's ready for production?

I pilot EVERY beer in 5 gallon batches until it is at least 90% of what I am looking and I know how to make up the remaining 10%. Most new beers are piloted for 4 – 9 months (many pilots are running simultaneously)

What style of beer is your bestseller and why do you think that is?

Our core Belgian-style Ales, primarily the Dubbel and Tripel, because nobody else does them locally.

Does glassware really make a difference?

100%

What's the real difference between a Porter and a Stout?

Every thumb is a finger, but not all fingers are thumbs – that is the difference.

How important is IBU when it comes to picking out a beer? Do customers need to pay attention to it?

IBU is the absolute worst indicator to put on a package or sign because it is meaningless and superlative. Adding 3 pounds/BBL of hops to a dry-hopping schedule adds "0 IBU", but adds a tremendous amount of hop character to a beer.

MAUI BREWING CO.

605 Lipoa Parkway
Kihei, HI 96753

Garrett W. Marrero

Typically, how much beer do you guys produce in an average year?

Approx 60,000 barrels of beer in addition to soda, canned cocktails, spirits and coffee

How much beer do you personally consume on an average workday?

Pre-covid zero, during covid 3-4 beers

What's your favorite food to eat with beer and why?

Honestly a great pizza and a pale ale.

About how much money does it cost to open a brewery?

Thats a very broad question. 50k -5mm comes to mind

What are today's worst beer trends?

Glitter, milkshake, adding sugar and adjuncts that'll referment and blow up

What beers are you best known for and why?

Coconut Hiwa Porter, we invented brewing with Coconut so thats what we're most well known for.

What sets your brewery apart from most others?

Authentic local Hawaiian beer, produced with nearly all grid-independent energy. Local, innovative, sustainability minded craft brewery if you will.

What are the biggest obstacles to continued craft beer growth?

Costs rising, margins shrinking. Big beer masquerading as craft.

How did you first discover craft beer and what made you want to enter the business?

Grandpa brought a keg of Stone IPA to my high school grad party

How do you attempt to increase beer production while still staying true to both your brand and your unique styles?

Efficiency, trial & error, equipment, automation

End of a long brew day, what are you drinking?

Right now? Mosaic Lite, a 100 calorie session ipa we brew.... then a gin & tonic

What style of beer is your bestseller and why do you think that is?

Bikini Blonde Lager, helles style lager crushable and flavorful. Great for Hawaii's weather and beaches

Does glassware really make a difference?

Yes without question.

How important is IBU when it comes to picking out a beer? Do customers need to pay attention to it?

No they don't, i'd say "perceived" ibu is more important. Todays craft beer drinker gravitates towards hoppy in the aromatic sense rather than bitterness.

MADCOW BREWING CO.

206 SE 166th Ave
Portland, OR 97233

Jason Blair
Owner/Head Brewer

Typically, how much beer do you guys produce in an average year?

Currently producing about 50 BBLs a year.

How much beer do you personally consume on an average workday?

0-2, depends on what I am doing.

What's your favorite food to eat with beer and why?

Anything grilled. I love how the grilling aspect of the food will bring out flavors in the beer.

About how much money does it cost to open a brewery?

Depends on the size and plan. We started as a 1 BBL brewery with plans of distribution only to start. In the next year we hope to open a tap room with a small kitchen. For us it was a start up cost of about $20,000.

What are today's worst beer trends?

Milkshake anything and the overly hazy IPA's

In the past few years we have seen a massive surge in the popularity of Hazy IPA's and Sours, what do you believe the next popular beer style will be?

A return to normalize beer flavors. Lagers, Pale Ale's, Scotch Ale's, English Ales.....

When you first opened the brewery, what was the biggest obstacle? What advice would you give someone thinking about opening a brewery to avoid some of the pitfalls you experienced?

Our biggest obstacle was the crowded Portland market. On top of that we started with packaging our beer instead of selling in kegs. Shelf space isn't too difficult, it is keeping that shelf space that is the real challenge. My advice would be to find a spot in your plan that you can open and operate on a smaller scale and grow organically. Especially during these times. Early pitfalls I would avoid is to try and stay away from making your beer too fast.....learn what you can from established brewers, we all are in this together, and make quality beer.

What beers are you best known for and why?

Saisons....we make some pretty good clean saisons. No brett, but we match the flavors and fermentation schedules pretty good.

What sets your brewery apart from most others?

We started as the smallest brewery in Oregon (there are a few others at 1 BBL now), and we do everything one at a time. One barrel at a time, one bottle/can at a time, one label at a time. It is a labor of love.

How do you decide on new beers to brew?

I typically start by tossing out ideas from customers or followers to see what the market would bear.

What are the biggest obstacles to continued craft beer growth?

Currently in 2020, it will be getting enough customers to return to the tap rooms.

What are the biggest problems you run into in producing beer?

Being small it is having too many styles in production at one time and not being able to keep them all in inventory.

How did you first discover craft beer and what made you want to enter the business?

I had my first introduction to craft beer from a friend who told me I just had to try this beer he found on draft. It was on Old Rasputin Imperial Stout from North Coast, I was hooked. I started homebrewing in 2002 and it quickly grew into a passion. In 2010, I helped a few breweries open in an area where there was zero to wet my whistle per say. In 2015/2016 I entered quite a few contests and took home quite a few medals and it was decided that we would make a go of it. We opened for business in June of 2017.

How do you attempt to increase beer production while still staying true to both your brand and your unique styles?

Social media posting right now. Opening a tap room to serve more of our customers and community soon.

What beer would you brew if cost, production, and sales were no object?

Lagers and barrel aged beer.

End of a long brew day, what are you drinking?

If it was a tough brew day, a light lager. Something easy drinking. If it was a normal, easy day, something hoppy.

When coming out with a new brew, how much experimentation do you try to get in before you say it's ready for production?

On our scale, any first time beer is an experiment that is ready for production. Over the next batches we may tweak it, but we sell through it.

What style of beer is your bestseller and why do you think that is?

Our best seller right now is our Evening Milking Stout. I think it does well for a few reasons. It is a milk stout so it fits with our brewery name, MadCow Brewing, and it is a real good balance of export stout and the milk stout. On it's heals is our Golden Guernsey Honey Rye Saison.

What's the real difference between a Porter and a Stout?

Funny I just wrote a little bit in our newsletter about the differences on our 3 dark beers we offer. These two styles are really blurred when it comes to the real differences..... porter more leans to the coffee notes, and stouts to the chocolate.

How important is IBU when it comes to picking out a beer? Do customers need to pay attention to it?

I think this is only important to the "beer snobs'" It shouldn't matter unless you are looking for something bitter. You can have a great IPA with a low IBU, and same with the other styles. When you are looking for an imperial stout, you are not looking at IBU, but those beers will have 70-100 IBU depending on the malt bill.

MCALLISTER BREWING COMPANY

810 Dickerson Rd
North Wales, PA 19454

Kate McAllister
Head of Operations/Owner

Typically, how much beer do you guys make in a year?

Last year I believe we produced about 300 barrels of beer. Not too bad considering it was our first full year being open.

What's your favorite food to eat with beer and why?

I guess my favorite food to pair with a beer would be a hot soft pretzel with a couple dipping sauces. There's just something about salty that goes with beer so well.

What are today's worst beer trends?

In my opinion today's worst beer trends are the heavily fruited whatever's. I feel you can't even really call them beer, they are more like an alcoholic smoothie.

What beer is your brewery best known for and why?

The beers we are best known for is our Shovel Buddy - New England IPA, our Gras Mähen - German Pilsner, and our Skook Water - stout, although we have come up with quite a few very popular beers besides those. Our most popular beer right now is our "This is 2020: Social Distancing Edition" which is a blood orange New England IPA.

What sets your brewery apart from most others?

I believe what sets our brewery apart from others is that we focus on more traditional type beers. One of the best things that I have experienced over this past year has been the loyalty of our many regular customers. Especially through this whole quarantine fiasco, our patrons have been amazing!

How important is IBU when it comes to picking out a beer? Do customers need to pay attention to it?

IBU is very important when picking out a beer, as, if you don't like bitter, you should not go with high IBU beers.

MICKEY FINNS BREWERY

345 N Milwaukee Ave
Libertyville, IL 60048

Brian Grano
The oldest brewpub in Illinois

Typically, how much beer do you guys make in a year?

1000 Barrels

How much beer do you personally consume on an average workday?

4-5 pints

What's your favorite food to eat with beer and why?

Anything really

About how much does it cost to open a brewery?

A shit ton.

What are today's worst beer trends?

Hazy IPA's

When you first opened the brewery, what was the biggest obstacle?

Cash

What advice would you give someone thinking about opening a brewery to avoid some pitfalls you experienced?

Have way more cash on hand than you think you'll need.

How do you decide on new beers to brew?

Try to stay seasonal (lighter in summer, darker in winter) plus try to provide what people are asking for, while mixing in in new styles like our Italian Pilsner.

How did you first discover craft beer and what made you want to enter the business?

20 years ago got into the beer after being invited to a beerfest. Then an amazing opportunity opened up in my hometown.

What beer would you brew if cost, production, and sales were no object?

We brew whatever we want - we don't let cost, production get in the way. Sales is another thing if it won't sell why brew it. We would do more barrel aged if we had more space to store them.

Does glassware really make a difference?

100%

What beer is your brewery best known for and why?

Santa's Magic Belgian Strong Ale - great beer, high abv, great glass, great logo, only out at Xmas - so it always kills.

End of a long brew day, what are you drinking?

Generally whatever is new - right now it's our hefe weizen and cerveza.

MOUNTAIN VALLEY BREWING

4220 Mountain Valley Rd
Axton, VA 24054

Peggy Donivan

Typically, how much beer do you guys produce in an average year?

We are still growing, but on average we produce about 110-120 barrels per year

How much beer do you personally consume on an average workday?

1-2 pints

About how much money does it cost to open a brewery?

We built our original 1.5 barrel brewery from scratch with 55-gallon SS drums in our garage. About 35K covered the brew house, consultant, tasting room and building additions.

What are today's worst beer trends?

None – we love all styles. Too many sours get a bit old though. We like variety.

When you first opened the brewery, what was the biggest obstacle? What advice would you give someone thinking about opening a brewery to avoid some of the pitfalls you experienced?

Be patient and plan for at least 12 months for TTB approval and possible local zoning approval. We are a farm brewery growing hops in a rural area so we are zoned agricultural, which eases up on many legalities such as zoning.

What beers are you best known for and why?

We try to use a lot of fresh local ingredients so some of our most popular beers are our Misty Pines Saison (Thai Basil and lemongrass); Blue Bolt (Blueberry Stout) and Kookie Rooster (Toasted Coconut Cream Ale).

What sets your brewery apart from most others?

Honestly, we're best known for not making a bad beer! It's rare that anyone leaves a selection on a flight and customers frequently comment that they just can't decide on what to order. Other than the beer, we are known for the breathtaking farm view and family atmosphere.

What are the biggest reasons for the continual growth of craft breweries?

Craft Breweries are really a community gather place; people need that sense of community.

How do you reach beyond the hardcore beer drinkers and into the general public to sell your beer?

We have a house pale ale called Vulture Roost. It's easy drinking, smooth and refreshing.

Is there a popular beer you make that you just don't really like but everyone else loves?

Not a big fan of lagers/pilsner but we understand the appeal so we make it.

End of a long brew day, what are you drinking?

Any one of our delicious IPAs or our raspberry/hibiscus sour!

What style of beer is your bestseller and why do you think that is?

Our house ale, Vulture Roost is versatile and definitely one we need to keep on tap. The other is our hard seltzer called "Notch Yo Beer". The seltzer is fantastic and appeals to a wide audience.

How important is IBU when it comes to picking out a beer? Do customers need to pay attention to it?

We took IBU off our menu as we thought it pushed people away from some very tasty and smooth brews.

MISKATONIC BREWING COMPANY

1000 N Frontage Rd Ste C
Darien, IL 60561

Josh Mowry
Co-Founder, Brewer, and President

Typically, how much beer do you guys make in a year?

1000 U.S. Barrels

How much beer do you personally consume on an average workday?

1-2 Pints

What's your favorite food to eat with beer and why?

Cheese, as it is the perfect pairing, absolutely blows wine away. The beer's carbonation scrubs the cheese off of your tongue to allow for a much more fresh pairing.

About how much does it cost to open a brewery?

If you're shooting for a 15 BBL Brewery about 1 million dollars.

What are today's worst beer trends?

Ticking a beer off your list of trying and then never returning to it. Beer is like songs and albums, you should want to return to the best of them to chew on them again and think about them.

When you first opened the brewery, what was the biggest obstacle? What advice would you give someone thinking about opening a brewery to avoid some pitfalls you experienced?

Making our voice heard in the crowd, and it still is our number one labor. Advice is always think about how you're going to communicate your ideas to the people, NEVER assume they'll just run right to your idea.

How do you decide on new beers to brew?

We have a huge list! So it's easy, the ideas area always moving through our mind, so whichever we think is seasonally appropriate and might be appreciated by the crowd.

How did you first discover craft beer and what made you want to enter the business?

I discovered it on a trip and realized beer could be like any other food or beverage, expressing lots of craft and thought.

What beer would you brew if cost, production, and sales were no object?

Baltic Porter and Barrel-Aged Wilds

Does glassware really make a difference?

The shape of glassware helps enhance, but usually does not make or break an experience.

What beer is your brewery best known for and why?

West Coast Wizard, our West Coast IPA, probably because we're one of the few focusing on that as our main IPA!

End of a long brew day, what are you drinking?

Hamm's lager or a cocktail. It's nice to take a break from the more intense stuff and just enjoy a straightforward refresher, or think about a different kind of alcohol.

MUDDY RIVER FARM BREWERY

15544 County Hwy 23
Unadilla, NY 13849

Jared Wood

Typically, how much beer do you guys make in a year?

We brew on a 3 BBL system and produce approximately 100 barrels per
year.

How much beer do you personally consume on an average workday?

This is our part time job. When I am working at the brewery, I consume
very little, as I am responsible for customers, staff and normal operation.
A few pints would be a lot on an average day. I wish it was more
sometimes!

What's your favorite food to eat with beer and why?

I tend to gravitate towards spicy food. I think a nice crisp IPA refreshes the pallet when you have that crazy mouth burn from chomping on a great chicken wing.

About how much does it cost to open a brewery?

$50k-100k for a small operation

What are today's worst beer trends?

I used to think the East Coast IPA were great when they first arrived on the seen in Vermont, but now they are out of control and monotonous. Too many Brewers overdo it with the cloudiness and sweetness.

When you first opened the brewery, what was the biggest obstacle? What advice would you give someone thinking about opening a brewery to avoid some pitfalls you experienced?

Equipment is always difficult, because stainless steel is really expensive. We run tight margins, so some items are still on my wishlist, such as a keg washer and another fermenter.

How do you decide on new beers to brew?

My audience and the season dictates what I brew.

How did you first discover craft beer and what made you want to enter the business?

Back in College in the 90's at Syracuse University. We would all buy six packs and trade them out while playing Pitch and listening to Rusted Root.....hahaha. years later we started a hop yard motivated by New York State policies. From there, we figured the profit was in the beer.

What beer would you brew if cost, production, and sales were no object?

Probably a barreled aged Imperial Stout aged on Cherries.

Does glassware really make a difference?

We exclusively use "beer can" glassware, as it fits our vibe. I think some glassware is pretentious and is sometimes used to pour a smaller volume, but charge a premium price. That annoys me!!!!

What beer is your brewery best known for and why?

Probably our Hellbender Black IPA, because it is delicious of course!

End of a long brew day, what are you drinking?

Honestly........probably a mixture of a fruity IPA and a craft hard cider. I always pour the cider first, so my last sip has a nice clean and sweet finish.

MASH MONKEYS BREWING COMPANY

920 U.S. Highway 1 Unit 1
Sebastian, FL 32958

Derek Gerry
Co-owner/ brewer/ keg ninjaneer/ yeast whisperer

Typically, how much beer do you guys produce in an average year?

300-350 bbls

How much beer do you personally consume on an average workday?

4 pints

What's your favorite food to eat with beer and why?

Chicken wings, cuz they are good.

About how much money does it cost to open a brewery?

What ever you think it is, double it.

What are today's worst beer trends?

Lactose everything! Packaging yeast trub and hop matter into cans and bottles.

In the past few years we have seen a massive surge in the popularity of Hazy IPA's and Sours, what do you believe the next popular beer style will be?

Pilsner

When you first opened the brewery, what was the biggest obstacle? What advice would you give someone thinking about opening a brewery to avoid some of the pitfalls you experienced?

What sets your brewery apart from most others?

We propagate all of our yeast in house for each beer per style. Specific water profiles.

How do you decide on new beers to brew?

We do what we want when we want to because we want to.

What are the biggest reasons for the continual growth of craft breweries?

Beats me.

What are the biggest obstacles to continued craft beer growth?

Tap space in bars and restaurants.

What are the biggest problems you run into in producing beer?

People who only drink hazy or lactose beers.

How do you reach beyond the hardcore beer drinkers and into the general public to sell your beer?

Funny names.

How did you first discover craft beer and what made you want to enter the business?

Living in Portland Maine, going into Grittys and 3 dollar deweys drinking allagash.

How do you attempt to increase beer production while still staying true to both your brand and your unique styles?

Get more Fermenter's.

What's the style most fun to brew?

For me it's Belgian style.

What beer would you brew if cost, production, and sales were no object?

The same things we make now.

Is there a popular beer you make that you just don't really like but everyone else loves?

Pastry stouts.

End of a long brew day, what are you drinking?

Kolsch Schwarzbier Vienna lager.

What are a few beers that other brewers are making that you really find impressive?

Barrel conditioned wild beers.

How do you feel the internet has changed the way the craft brewing industry operates?

It's ok to be an ass clown.

When coming out with a new brew, how much experimentation do you try to get in before you say it's ready for production?

Depends on how far out the box it is.

What style of beer is your bestseller and why do you think that is?

Acqua Pazza IPA.

Does glassware really make a difference?

Yup!

What's the real difference between a Porter and a Stout?

Experience.

How important is IBU when it comes to picking out a beer?

Do customers need to pay attention to it? Only if they can't handle it.

MIDDLETON BREWING (MBTX)

101 Oakwood Loop
San Marcos, TX 78666

Carl Rabenaldt

Typically, how much beer do you guys make in a year?

750 Barrels per year.

How much beer do you personally consume on an average workday?

2 beers per day.

What's your favorite food to eat with beer and why?

All kinds but fried foods or BBQ are my favorite. Probably because of the spiciness.

About how much does it cost to open a brewery?

That is difficult to answer. Are you opening a microbrewery at 5bbls or something like a 40bbl system. Will you have a tap room or only wholesalebeer. The cost could be anywhere between $100,000 to $4,000,000. Of course the numbers could be much larger if you are seeking to become a venue for events such as weddings.

What are today's worst beer trends?

Non-alcoholic beer.

When you first opened the brewery, what was the biggest obstacle?

Understanding that a successful brewery is as much about beer production as it is about business processes.

What advice would you give someone thinking about opening a brewery to avoid some pitfalls you experienced?

Don't think that because you can brew a great beer that you can run a successful business. Don't be afraid to seek advice.

How do you decide on new beers to brew?

We have 5 mainstays that don't change much. We then have 12 tap handles that are either rotating (seasonal) beer we brew or new beer. At any one time, we try to have at least one new beer on the tap wall. We make these decisions by what we read and discuss with the stakeholders of the business.

How did you first discover craft beer and what made you want to enter the business?

Probably from visiting other breweries over a period of time. I developed a thirst for real craft beer. It was also what all the cool kids were doing

What beer would you brew if cost, production, and sales were no object?

We don't think about these things when brewing beer; we focus on brewing great beers. We do think about cost, production and sales when it comes to the business side. We constantly try to think of ways to cut cost in the business such as reducing cost of electricity or buying grain in bulk. We would never consider purchasing cheaper grain or any other ingredient to reduce price.

Does glassware really make a difference?

The craft beer industry is as much about the experience as it is the taste of beer. Glassware is very important. Not only is the glassware important but having a "beer clean" glass is equally important. Drinking out of the wrong glass or plastic is just not the same. We will only serve in glass!

What beer is your brewery best known for and why?

Great craft beer, relaxed attitude and vibrant sounds.

End of a long brew day, what are you drinking?

A new England IPA.

METRIC BREWING COMPANY

1213 N Circle Dr
Colorado Springs, CO 80909

Morgan Perry
Taproom Manager

Typically, how much beer do you guys make in a year?

Around 300 Barrels.

How much beer do you personally consume on an average workday?

Depends, sometimes a beer or two, other times we will go a day or two in-between servings. It's easy to have a beer each day.

What's your favorite food to eat with beer and why?

Tacos! Easy to pair with most tappings.

About how much does it cost to open a brewery?

The cost is variable, depending on how much work you intend to put in yourself. Hiring to build can be expensive.

What are today's worst beer trends?

N/A

When you first opened the brewery, what was the biggest obstacle? What advice would you give someone thinking about opening a brewery to avoid some pitfalls you experienced?

The biggest obstacle for us was scheduling consistent food trucks (we do not have a kitchen on site) and learning how often to brew again. As you open a brewery, it takes time to learn what the customer trends are, which beers are consumed that quickest and how often one should have beers (kegs) on deck ready to go. Running out of beer is the worst thing for a brewery, as you need to pour beer to pay the bills. I am still learning each day, and I have no doubt that I will continue to do so.

How do you decide on new beers to brew?

My brother (the brewer and co-owner) is in charge of the brew schedule. We plan for different seasonal offerings, certain fan favorites. We also just brainstorm and try to be as creative as we can. You can't always brew what "you" like to drink—it's about the community and paying attention to trends and listening to your patrons.

How did you first discover craft beer and what made you want to enter the business?

My brother worked in the lab at the BSI (Brew Science Institute), following that, he ran the lab and was the assistant brewer at Bristol Brewing prior to opening Metric Brewing.

What beer would you brew if cost, production, and sales were no object?

More Schwarzbiers and Lagers. We brew on a smaller system, and It's unrealistic for us to tie up tanks for weeks at a time.

Does glassware really make a difference?

Glassware absolutely makes a difference.

What beer is your brewery best known for and why?

Raspberry Kolsch, Hazy IPA, Coffee Milk Stout, variety of Sour Beers. They just happen to be fan favorites. All delicious.

End of a long brew day, what are you drinking?

Saisons, West Coast IPAs, Belgians... there's usually a favorite pour on tap that we gravitate towards.

MACON BEER COMPANY

345 Oglethorpe St
Macon, GA 31201

Typically, how much beer do you guys make in a year?

We produce about 3,000-4,000 barrels a year and it's been increasing.

How much beer do you personally consume on an average workday?

Very little. I'll probably have a beer or two on a Friday or Saturday night. I don't think it wise to consume beer while working in the brewery. There are a lot of chemicals, forklifts, hot water, and other dangerous items about, so it isn't too smart to be inebriated around that stuff.

What's your favorite food to eat with beer and why?

Pizza. A pizza and a pint are the perfect pair.

About how much does it cost to open a brewery?

A whole lot more than people think. It depends on the size of the brewery, but anywhere from 500,000 upward for a barebones operation.

What are today's worst beer trends?

Fruit bombs. Beers that taste like cocktails and other alcoholic beverages. It's okay to put fruit in beer, but beer shouldn't taste like an alcoholic fruit juice. There should be a taste of malt, hops, yeast, and beer flavors. It shouldn't be a carbonated cocktail with more adjunct than traditional beer ingredients. Innovation is great, but innovation shouldn't be covering up beer flavors with fruits, syrups, and other crap.

When you first opened the brewery, what was the biggest obstacle? What advice would you give someone thinking about opening a brewery to avoid some pitfalls you experienced?

The biggest obstacle was being the new kid on the block in a scene full of traditional WASP type brewers who were older and bearded. So it brought a lot of opposition and phone calls from the Department of Revenue because somebody would have "anonymously" complained about something I allegedly was doing, that I really wasn't. The biggest advice I would give is to not give into the "brewer community" myth too much, because the scene isn't as friendly as folks make it out to be for seemingly non-traditional brewers. Focus on yourself, your craft, and your crew. Keep your nose to the grindstone and don't let the detractors bring you down.

How do you decide on new beers to brew?

We find inspiration from all places. Sometimes when I'm eating a meal I'll think about a beer that'll complement the food. Sometimes while hanging out with my friends we talk about the type of beer we would like drink. So it really depends, but usually it comes from within naturally, or from friends while talking.

How did you first discover craft beer and what made you want to enter the business?

I first discovered it at a pizza place while in college. I drank a Dogfishhead 90 minute IPA, I know a bold beginning to craft brew, because I thought the name was cool. What made me want to enter the business was the communal aspect of beer and the friendships that are created around a pint.

What beer would you brew if cost, production, and sales were no object?

The ones I'm brewing now.

Does glassware really make a difference?

It does. Simple as that. Some glassware helps you smell and taste the beer better.

What beer is your brewery best known for and why?

Macon Progress Pale Ale, because it's a simple easy drinking pale ale that everybody can enjoy. It's a classic.

End of a long brew day, what are you drinking?

Goldtop IPA. It's a clean and crisp IPA without any frills or adjuncts.

MISSING FALLS BREWERY

540 S Main St Bldg 1 Ste 112
Akron, OH 44311

Will Myers
COO

Typically, how much beer do you guys make in a year?

Approximately 400 bbl's

How much beer do you personally consume on an average workday?

1 pint

What's your favorite food to eat with beer and why?

A good pizza. It just seems they were meant to go together.

About how much does it cost to open a brewery?

Depends on the size. I'd say $500k minimum if you aren't cutting corners

What are today's worst beer trends?

I'm personally tired of NEIPA's

When you first opened the brewery, what was the biggest obstacle? What advice would you give someone thinking about opening a brewery to avoid some pitfalls you experienced?

The location. Don't just pick a building to put your brewery in for location, but rather find one that already has the utilities in place at levels you will need. 3 phase power, large enough water supply, etc. You will save tons of money.

How do you decide on new beers to brew?

Our Brewmaster and Head Brewer bump their heads together repeatedly until a good idea falls out.

How did you first discover craft beer and what made you want to enter the business?

I met one of my partners through work who turned me onto homebrewing. We got a bit carried away and the next thing you know we had a $5k homebrewing system and a walk-in cooler in the garage. We would make so much beer that we would share it with anyone we could. The feedback was incredible so we decided to give it a go. Our original plans were not quite as extensive as what we ended up doing in the end.

What beer would you brew if cost, production, and sales were no object?

I love bourbon barrel aged beers so I think a HUGE BBA stout.

Does glassware really make a difference?

Yes, I believe so, though not as much as people claim it does.

What beer is your brewery best known for and why?

Terror of the 7 - C's. It won the Silver Medal at the Ohio Craft Brewers Cup in 2019. People love IPA's and this is a big one. 7.7% ABV and 177IBU's

End of a long brew day, what are you drinking?

Water. The drive home is not short. That's funny. Before we opened a brewery, the answer would have been beer.

MOUNTAIN FORK BREWERY

89 N Lukfata Trail Rd
Broken Bow, OK 74728

Typically, how much beer do you guys produce in an average year?

1k

How much beer do you personally consume on an average workday?

Less than a pint

What's your favorite food to eat with beer and why?

Spicy / salty / savory - pairs best

About how much money does it cost to open a brewery?

2 Million or 200k & lot of b/s/t

What are today's worst beer trends?

Every palate is unique and correct

In the past few years we have seen a massive surge in the popularity of Hazy IPA's and Sours, what do you believe the next popular beer style will be?

Back to the Core (s)

When you first opened the brewery, what was the biggest obstacle? What advice would you give someone thinking about opening a brewery to avoid some of the pitfalls you experienced?

Learn the tradecraft & take care of your contractors. Hire vetted professional consultants. Even if do not use their advice. Listen.

What beers are you best known for and why?

Cores

What sets your brewery apart from most others?

Travel destination

How do you decide on new beers to brew?

Customer feedback, market, mad scientist

What are the biggest reasons for the continual growth of craft breweries?

Support local - desire to spend personal money on local

What are the biggest obstacles to continued craft beer growth?

Education transparency

How do you reach beyond the hardcore beer drinkers and into the general public to sell your beer?

Education tastings transparency

How did you first discover craft beer and what made you want to enter the business?

Home brewing

How do you attempt to increase beer production while still staying true to both your brand and your unique styles?

Long days - recalibrate with a beer at the end

What's the style most fun to brew?

The one that keeps the lights on

What beer would you brew if cost, production, and sales were no object?

Same we do - variety is spice of life & why we have seasons

Is there a popular beer you make that you just don't really like but everyone else loves?

Sours

End of a long brew day, what are you drinking?

Light if hot , dark otherwise

What are a few beers that other brewers are making that you really find impressive?

Brut , barrel aged, light & hoppy, innovation ingredients

How do you feel the internet has changed the way the craft brewing industry operates?

Helps showcase new beers to wider audience

When coming out with a new brew, how much experimentation do you try to get in before you say it's ready for production?

LOTS ... more data better data

What style of beer is your bestseller and why do you think that is?

Belgian golden - light clean and 8.9%

Does glassware really make a difference?

Yes - also glass rinsers , lacing is beautiful

What's the real difference between a Porter and a Stout?

Malt and abv

How important is IBU when it comes to picking out a beer? Do customers need to pay attention to it?

Not so much, more trust in brewery and style guidelines yes to pay attention, every brewery lil different

MODIST BREWING COMPANY

505 N 3rd St
Minneapolis, MN 55401

Keigan Knee
Co-Founder & Flavor Overlord "Director of Product Development"

Typically, how much beer do you guys make in a year?

5500bbl

How much beer do you personally consume on an average workday?

1.5 pints

What's your favorite food to eat with beer and why?

Pizza. Pizza is god and pairs so well with many beer styles

About how much does it cost to open a brewery?

Depending on the scope of the the project 75k to millions

What are today's worst beer trends?

Still the same as it has been for ages. Poorly quality beer, with off flavors and flaws sold to unknowing customers.

When you first opened the brewery, what was the biggest obstacle?

Dialing in our brewhouse to optimize efficiency and performance.

What advice would you give someone thinking about opening a brewery to avoid some pitfalls you experienced?

Choose your business partners wisely for the long term, and make sure your floors self drain without creating pools of water.

How do you decide on new beers to brew?

Balancing innovation, flavors and styles to keep a variety of different options.

How did you first discover craft beer and what made you want to enter the business?

Fell into it by chance at my at the time neighborhood microbrewery. Discovered that my natural skill sets and passion for innovation was needed in the growing MN craft beer industry.

What beer would you brew if cost, production, and sales were no object?

Fortunately we get to brew the beers we want to brew already. From foeder lagers to barrel aged beers. We created Modist Brewing to discover what beer can be while committing to our high quality standards throughout the company.

Does glassware really make a difference?

Yes. First and foremost a clean glass is the best glass. Glassware amplifies the drinking experience of each beer in its own way. I like glassware that concentrates aroma for most beers and tall and skinny glasses for lagers.

What beer is your brewery best known for and why?

Dreamyard- our flagship IPA. It is very unique and is brewed with only wheat and oat malt and hopped generously with our hand selected Citra and Sultana hops.

End of a long brew day, what are you drinking?

A bit of everything and then one thousand foeder lagers.

MT LOWE BREWING COMPANY

150 E Saint Joseph St
Arcadia, CA 91006

Cami Nemanich

Typically, how much beer do you guys produce in an average year?

About 1000 barrels

How much beer do you personally consume on an average workday?

1-2 pints

What's your favorite food to eat with beer and why?

Any food with a really good craft beer lol

About how much money does it cost to open a brewery?

Depending on the size and decor 200k-5mil. Us personally 400k

What are today's worst beer trends?

Hard seltzer

In the past few years we have seen a massive surge in the popularity of Hazy IPA's and Sours, what do you believe the next popular beer style will be?

Light easy drinking low abv beers

When you first opened the brewery, what was the biggest obstacle? What advice would you give someone thinking about opening a brewery to avoid some of the pitfalls you experienced?

Getting our licenses. We would say now is not the time to open as the market is flooded with breweries

What beers are you best known for and why?

Our Honey Hef and our Hazy IPA (the Lowe Down)

What sets your brewery apart from most others?

We are family friendly and community driven.

How do you decide on new beers to brew?

We follow the trends to a point and then we let our patrons suggest what they'd like

What are the biggest reasons for the continual growth of craft breweries?

So big beer doesn't have the monopoly and it helps small business owners have an opportunity to make their own mark

What are the biggest obstacles to continued craft beer growth?

To stay fresh and relevant as the trends are consistently changing along with big beer buying up craft breweries so they can disguise themselves as "craft"

What are the biggest problems you run into in producing beer?

We run out of tanks to ferment new beers

How do you reach beyond the hardcore beer drinkers and into the general public to sell your beer?

We like to think if mama's happy then the men and families will come and support so we make sure to always have options for the ladies who are not hardcore craft beer enthusiasts

How did you first discover craft beer and what made you want to enter the business?

We loved beer and making beer was a hobby. We were tired of our jobs and wanted to do something we love and enjoy doing.

How do you attempt to increase beer production while still staying true to both your brand and your unique styles?

We do small batches of different brews to test out and if they hit we'll make more!

What's the style most fun to brew?

Experimental brews

What beer would you brew if cost, production, and sales were no object?

We honestly don't have a style that we're the most fond of. We like all beer and like to try new brews all the time.

Is there a popular beer you make that you just don't really like but everyone else loves?

A Pilsner

End of a long brew day, what are you drinking?

By the end of the brew.. something light

What are a few beers that other brewers are making that you really find impressive?

Barrel aged sours

How do you feel the internet has changed the way the craft brewing industry operates?

Social media definitely is the way of advertising

When coming out with a new brew, how much experimentation do you try to get in before you say it's ready for production?

Well if it doesn't taste like we imagined we tweak it till we like it and call it something else

What style of beer is your bestseller and why do you think that is?

Our light easy drinking beers sell the best.

Does glassware really make a difference?

In our experience, no.

What's the real difference between a Porter and a Stout?

The percentage of alcohol

How important is IBU when it comes to picking out a beer? Do customers need to pay attention to it?

Some do but not all. For us it's very important as some like high IBUs and some prefer super low IBUs

MAD MALTS BREWERY & TAP ROOM

109 Maple Ave NW
Huntsville, AL 35801

Chris

Typically, how much beer do you guys make in a year?

MM normally runs about 500 bbls a year.

How much beer do you personally consume on an average workday?

Not as much as most people think, maybe a pint every other day, or less.

What's your favorite food to eat with beer and why?

Most meats; steaks, pork chops, hamburgers, sausages, even chicken (grilled). The malts and hops just mix well with the fats and char on meat for me.

About how much does it cost to open a brewery?

As long as you are not adding a restaurant, it's not hugely expensive. A real brewery, looking at about $400k to $600k, depending on location.

What are today's worst beer trends?

Worst one now "What's new TODAY?" That trend is making Brewers put out new beers that don't have any thought behind em, just dump something trendy in the beer and ship it.

When you first opened the brewery, what was the biggest obstacle? What advice would you give someone thinking about opening a brewery to avoid some pitfalls you experienced?

I have opened 3 breweries, each time it was a different problem:

1) licensing and approvals will take forever, 6 months minimum start to finish (if you know what you are doing).

2) don't mess with the City! Don't argue with code, you piss off the city or county and they will make your life hell. It's their signature, and they know it. Plus most of those stupid rules are there from others doing stupid things that have impacted the city. Just listen, talk and do.

3) partners. I'll just leave it at have an iron-clad partner agreement and DON'T partner with a friend...

How do you decide on new beers to brew?

I love flavors and beer, so experiment a lot. Nothing goes out without my taste approval also. I may not like something one of my guys makes, but if it's a solid flavor and not a fad, it goes to the Tap Room for testing before it goes out.

How did you first discover craft beer and what made you want to enter the business?

A long time ago, before cell phones and electricity, I loved to cook, beers, and flavors. I also loved German beers, which got me into Belgian beers, which got me into Craft beers. I found a book xxx by Charlie P, and then joined my local craft club, Rocket City Brewers. A bunch of us were talking about beers and Alabama laws and we came up with "if the laws change, we should open up a brewery". Well they did and 6 of us opened a Brewery.

What beer would you brew if cost, production, and sales were no object?

Never ran into this concept before, because cost, production, and sales don't normally limit me, honestly. I have released beers that violate all three of the above. In small batches though!

Does glassware really make a difference?

Not to any real level of perception in the market. Real impact is beer line cleanliness, glass cleanliness, temperature of the beer at delivery to the person, consistency of the beer, and server attitude.

What beer is your brewery best known for and why?

We are known for our Vanilla Porter and our Raspberry Blonde. Both beers trade for the 1 spot in both the tap room and retail. Vanilla Porter is a Robust English style porter, rich and Smith with a great vanilla background. Raspberry Blonde is light tasting, honey and raspberry bomb, very refreshing, with an 8.5% ABV kick.

End of a long brew day, what are you drinking?

Either a Moonbounce golden rye or a sour.

MAD JACK'S MOUNTAIN BREWERY

23 Main Street
Bailey, CO 80421

Jack Hansell

Typically, how much beer do you guys produce in an average year?

200 bbl

How much beer do you personally consume on an average workday?

32 oz

What's your favorite food to eat with beer and why?

Most anything. Beer is the perfect pairing due to varieties, styles, flavors
which can compliment, cut or cleanse the pallet

About how much money does it cost to open a brewery?

I am a brewery consultant and working on a project at this time for a 50,000 bbl brewery. Cost estimates range from $20-25M at this point. This question has so many variables it is hard to answer properly.

What are today's worst beer trends?

Major players are seeing mid single digit declines in their core brands. Thus they are buying up craft breweries and diminishing the true nature of craft. Craft volumes are on the rise albeit slower than past years.

In the past few years we have seen a massive surge in the popularity of Hazy IPA's and Sours, what do you believe the next popular beer style will be?

I believe it will be a couple of directions.

1. CBD and possibly THC infused beers.

2. A return to traditional styles with a focus on hitting the profiles

3. Grain to Glass purity

When you first opened the brewery, what was the biggest obstacle? What advice would you give someone thinking about opening a brewery to avoid some of the pitfalls you experienced?

1. Funding. Ensure you have plenty of backing to support 3-5 years of operation.

2. Professional Services – make sure you have a solid CPA and Lawyer that knows brewing

What beers are you best known for and why?

1. ManJoeHobbsenero Blonde. This is a mango habanero blonde ale with just the right amount of late heat and great flavor ~5.5% ABV. By far our best seller.

2. Lions Head IPA – Well balanced IPA with ~60 IBU, ~ 7.2% ABV.

3. Antero Amber Ale – Smooth malty flavors balanced with just the right amount of hops. ~ 7% ABV ~ 40 IBU

What sets your brewery apart from most others?

We are a small mountain community brewery located on US 285 in Bailey, CO. We offer a wide selection of beers that rotate and are never exactly the same. Excellent outdoor seating with mountain views, Dog and Family Friendly. We offer hand made Paninis that satisfy your hunger. We are MAD about Beer! tm

How do you decide on new beers to brew?

Customer Feedback and Brewers desire to explore new ideas

What are the biggest reasons for the continual growth of craft breweries?

Wide variety of styles, flavors, and innovation

What are the biggest obstacles to continued craft beer growth?

Economic issues, ie Covid-19 and Big Brewers

What are the biggest problems you run into in producing beer?

Lack of Capacity

How do you reach beyond the hardcore beer drinkers and into the general public to sell your beer?

We are not after the typical light beer drinkers. We rely on word of mouth, social media and beer app ratings.

How did you first discover craft beer and what made you want to enter the business?

15+ years working for Molson Coors, 30+ years homebrewing. During my time at MC I had the opportunity to go through brewing school, which focused on beer science and engineering. We trained at craft as well as commercial breweries. I fell in love with the craft side

How do you attempt to increase beer production while still staying true to both your brand and your unique styles?

This is tough for us. We need an infusion of investment to allow us to expand capacity

What's the style most fun to brew?

Berliner Weiss. We produce this with fresh berries of the season and explore.

What beer would you brew if cost, production, and sales were no object?

All of our current portfolio, IPA, Man Joe, Berliner Weiss, Hefe Weissen, Stouts, Porters, Lagers

Is there a popular beer you make that you just don't really like but everyone else loves?

Nope

End of a long brew day, what are you drinking?

Beer and perhaps a scotch

What are a few beers that other brewers are making that you really find impressive?

Too many to mention.

How do you feel the internet has changed the way the craft brewing industry operates?

Social Media of course. But primarily people can research how beer is made, what happens during the process, and are much more knowledgeable about styles

When coming out with a new brew, how much experimentation do you try to get in before you say it's ready for production?

1-2 home brew batches and sampling with our customers.

What style of beer is your bestseller and why do you think that is?

See above. Man Joe Hobbsenero. The story behind the name as well as the great beer itself.

Does glassware really make a difference?

It can but generally this is unique to big brands such as Stella Artois, Guiness etc.

What's the real difference between a Porter and a Stout?

Stouts will have a more coffee note vs a Porter. Difference in grains used is the driver. Porters typically use dark malted barley and stouts use a roasted unmalted barley.

How important is IBU when it comes to picking out a beer? Do customers need to pay attention to it?

Many don't really understand what IBU stands for. Many ask for the least hoppy beer or in some cases "how hoppy is it".

NATURAL STATE BEER COMPANY

5214 W. Village Parkway, Suite 140
Rogers, AR 72758

Typically, how much beer do you guys make in a year?

We are just starting out and anticipate 300 BBL this year

About how much does it cost to open a brewery?

Loaded question, way too many variables to provide a number.

When you first opened the brewery, what was the biggest obstacle? What advice would you give someone thinking about opening a brewery to avoid some pitfalls you experienced?

Permitting and cost are the two biggest hurdles. Do your research and find the right partners and money.

How do you decide on new beers to brew?

Collaboration with owners and brewers.

How did you first discover craft beer and what made you want to enter the business?

Homebrewing was introduced to me by my brother and that opened the world to craft beer for me.

Does glassware really make a difference?

Absolutely, your first sense in consuming a beer is your sense of sight. The right beer in the right glass not only looks sexy, but tastes better.

What beer is your brewery best known for and why?

European Lagers all kinds, but our Helles is fantastic and a top seller.

End of a long brew day, what are you drinking?

Helles Lager, light refreshing and popular among many brewers. Something I can have multiples of.

NORTH JETTY BREWING

4200 Pacific Way
Seaview, WA 98644

Erik Svendsen

Typically, how much beer do you guys make in a year?

Pre-COVID approximately 1,000 barrels

How much beer do you personally consume on an average workday?

Less that one pint.

What's your favorite food to eat with beer and why?

Tacos - great combo

About how much does it cost to open a brewery?

More than you expect at the beginning and it goes up from there. Have twice as much as you think you need. If at all possible buy your facility rather than lease.

What are today's worst beer trends?

Glitter beer, desert beer.

When you first opened the brewery, what was the biggest obstacle? What advice would you give someone thinking about opening a brewery to avoid some pitfalls you experienced?

Make sure you decide who you want to be. Brewpub, local taproom, production facility, draft heavy vs. package heavy.

How do you decide on new beers to brew?

Look at what is hot in the market, work with our head brewery to discuss what would be a good beer to bring to market.

How did you first discover craft beer and what made you want to enter the business?

I started home-brewing in college in 1996. I was a CPA and just sort of fell into the brewery ownership role. It may be a longer story than you have time for, but a restaurant in our little beach town wanted their own beer on tap in 2012. I got involved and it spiraled into North Jetty Brewing from there.

What beer would you brew if cost, production, and sales were no object?

West Coast IPAs

Does glassware really make a difference?

Depends on what experience you are looking for.If you want a refreshing pint after working in the yard all day - probably not. If you are looking to enjoy every nuance of a barrel-aged spontaneous ferment then probably so.

What beer is your brewery best known for and why?

Leadbetter Red Scottish-Style Ale. We are in a tourist beach town. We cater to fairly rural beer drinkers and urban tourists coming from Seattle and Portland areas. Our Leadbetter Red is easy-drinking and approachable for all, but with enough nuance to keeps "fanboy" happy.

End of a long brew day, what are you drinking?

Bourbon or an Agave spirit.

NAILERS BREWING COMPANY

6001 N US Highway 31
Whiteland, IN 46184

Typically, how much beer do you guys produce in an average year

We are a small brewery and we only Brew around 50 barrels to 80 barrels here

How much beer do you personally consume on an average workday?

Maybe one

About how much money does it cost to open a brewery?

The false narrative that it takes $1 million to open up a brewery is total rubbish. We opened our brewery for less than $80,000 looking back if you only wanna open the tap room you could do it for less than 30,000 but you must do it all yourself like I did.

The biggest expense you're gonna have is the walk in cooler and kegs everything else can be done homebrew style size.

What are today's worst beer trends?

What is today's worst beer trends well, if we're talking about beer itself I don't think there is one , if we're talking about what people do to craft beer I think there's a lot of them. One of those terrible trends is these beer apps! All these beer apps to rate people for beer I think is a terrible idea because every brewery and brewmaster has their own flavor and the beer apps are giving people little badges to rate beer to their taste. Most of the people that I have interviewed watching them in my taphouse rate my beer has never made a beer. And a lot of these beer people follow those apps and they never get to taste good beer because one person don't like that beer and I think that is a terrible model and it does hurt businesses!! You just have to remember you brew what tastes good to you first then you listen to your customers and you change for your customers and if you're going to open most breweries fail due to not listening to their customers! " It's not your beer anymore it's the customers beer"

In the past few years we have seen a massive surge in the popularity of Hazy IPA's and Sours, what do you believe the next popular beer style will be?

I think anything that is dank and weird and has multiple flavors I think that's the next craze And it doesn't necessarily have to have any alcohol whatsoever

When you first opened the brewery, what was the biggest obstacle?

Our biggest obstacle with opening was the amount of help that you need because whatever you think will not fail will fail. Our biggest obstacle was our POS system not enough of them, Internet crashing due to free Wi-Fi for customers at 300 people logging onto one router.

What advice would you give someone thinking about opening a brewery to avoid some of the pitfalls you experienced?

1.Make sure every single person understands and knows completely your POS system.

2. Make sure every single person does not deviate from their job.

3. Make sure you have plenty of CO_2.

4. Make sure you have someone at the door checking drivers license.

5. Make sure you have a plan to hold three times more than your capacity if you cannot let them in , make sure you have signs were everybody needs to be.

6. Make sure you have a good accountant.

7. Make sure you take your time make sure you have fun and most of all make sure that the owner is greeting public and don't forget your wife because you just drug her into this thing.!!!!!

8.. The most important is to make sure you know every single thing to do in that business and you could do it by yourself.

9. Second most important is do not follow trends (create them) This is your business this is your dream don't follow someone else's dream and just be a copycat!!!!! Have fun

What beers are you best known for and why?

We are known for blueberry Pilz tangerine ale and peanut butter Stout we are told that we do it better than anyone else

What sets your brewery apart from most others?

1. One we offer food,

2. We have a one-man show so if Something Happens one man can still continue running the brewery

How do you decide on new beers to brew?

We brew what people want to drink ,we do not follow what people are doing outside of the brewery when they come into the brewery they say hey you know what would be good is this this this and this we listen to everyone then i make a decision when I want to brew something

What are the biggest reasons for the continual growth of craft breweries?

I personally think people are getting tired of the big three and the younger generation is appreciating homegrown

What are the biggest problems you run into in producing beer?

I am too small can't supply enough of the beers that people want to drink.

How did you first discover craft beer and what made you want to enter the business?

My youngest son love drinking beer, I however did not many years ago. He wanted me to keep buying him the big three beer and one day I refused and said if you want it you make it and we started making beer and we thought we would go ahead and open up a brewery so I could retire from my previous job.

How do you attempt to increase beer production while still staying true to both your brand and your unique styles?

Go slow don't go fast don't worry about demand to stay true to yourself keep it manageable , the bigger you are the harder you fall.

Is there a popular beer you make that you just don't really like but everyone else loves?

I like to Brew all the beer so there really isn't one that I don't like to brew.

End of a long brew day, what are you drinking?

An easy drinking Pilsner.

How do you feel the internet has changed the way the craft brewing industry operates?

This question I'll have to refer back to the beer apps.

When coming out with a new brew, how much experimentation do you try to get in before you say it's ready for production?

Here at our brewery we do not do that. We see something in our head we just do it and how it turns out is how it turns out . If it's totally not good then will ditch it , if not then we put it out on the tap.

What style of beer is your bestseller and why do you think that is?

Our best seller is a blueberry Pilsner it's light it's fruity and it's just plain refreshing at any time of the year.

Does glassware really make a difference?

Absolutely not.

What's the real difference between a Porter and a Stout?

To me coffee flavor versus a roasted barley flavor.

How important is IBU when it comes to picking out a beer? Do customers need to pay attention to it?

I think it's very important I think it's more important than ABV. If you'd like a light beer stay below 20 , if you like something with a little Thang go above 20, and if you'd like a big beer stay above 50.

Any final words?

So to reiterate opening a brewery you have to remember this it is not your beer anymore. Don't follow trends create them, listen to your customers, prepare for the worst hope for the best, get volunteers because you cannot count on people to follow your dream, and don't put all your eggs in one basket.

And about my Brewery we are a three barrel system
(5) - 3 barrel fermentors
(80) - 5gallon kegs
(20) - 15gl kegs
16x8 walk-in cooler
2400 sqft total sqft
1/2 brewery - 1/2 tap house
16x10 kitchen with no hood
and we can hold 72 people
with 15 at the bar

NAKED RIVER BREWING

1791 Reggie White Blvd,
Chattanooga, TN 37408

Jake Raulston
President

Nathan Woods
Head Brewer

Typically, how much beer do you guys produce in an average year?

Nathan - In 2018 we opened the doors in November and made a splash with a small amount of production. In 2019 we produced just over 1,200bbls and in 2020 we had planned to produce 2,400bbl. We will probably finish the year around 1,800bbls due to Covid-19.

How much beer do you personally consume on an average workday?

Jake - (4-5)

Nathan - As the head brewer: I typically am the one to walk people through beer, or to sample out of tanks... 4-5/ workday

What's your favorite food to eat with beer and why?

Jake - Brats or beer cheese with spent grain pretzels

Nathan - As the head brewer it's all about the pairing. I enjoy having a beer with all types of foods. My favorite is the best compliment to both beer and food. I do really love nachos and pizza with a refreshing Lager or IPA.

About how much money does it cost to open a brewery?

Jake - Beer only, about 25-50k per bbl system

Nathan - Double all your estimates haha, depending on serving and packaging equipment/ styles the skys the limit. In order for us to open Naked River Brewing Company many of us had to quit our other jobs, or move to make this dream come true. One of the hardest start up costs is making sure you are in a position to quit jobs to work 70+hour weeks. (Hopefully to be at least paid in beer).

What are today's worst beer trends?

Jake - Nothing against seltzers, but can we stop calling them beers?

Nathan - I know they are good, but I really cannot stand heavy milkshake styled beers or food based beers. To me I think that some things definitely do not belong in a beer. For example fried chicken, pizza, hot sauce, or even whole cakes and pies.

In the past few years we have seen a massive surge in the popularity of Hazy IPA's and Sours, what do you believe the next popular beer style will be?

Jake - Low calorie, but double hopped IPAS

Nathan - I agree and echo the low calorie IPAs, but I also believe people are trending back to light crisp beers, typically light lagers. Before Covid-19 we saw a trend in big doubles and west coast IPAs growing.

When you first opened the brewery, what was the biggest obstacle? What advice would you give someone thinking about opening a brewery to avoid some of the pitfalls you experienced?

Jake - Get a contractor who has done a brewery before, and don't forget the Kegs! We forgot about all the kegs we would need in the initial budget

Nathan - I feel like we have killer space and building, but it was one of our biggest obstacles. Leave yourself plenty of room for expansion, even if you don't think you need it. Also, make sure you have good connections with suppliers you're interested in. Raw ingredients, safety equipment, chemicals, and befriend a plumber and electrician as soon as you can.

What beers are you best known for and why?

Jake - Moonpie stout - cause we crush 500lbs of moonpies to make this ridiculous beer

Nathan - We are absolutely best known for our Moonpie Stout. We are the only licensed brewery to use the Moonpie trademark. We get fresh moonpies straight from the bakery and then hand crush 500lbs per batch that we produce. Not only is this beer a huge hit in Chattanooga (and Tennessee), but people see and recognize the nostalgic logo nationwide.

What sets your brewery apart from most others?

Jake - The unique space and environment

Nathan - Not only do we offer more seating and space than most brewpubs, but we have very intelligent and friendly bar staff, we also offer exceptional beer and BBQ. To go along with our amazing beer and food we also work with the community to be a part of as many local events and collaborations as possible. This includes our ever rotating River Series IPAs. Our River Series are ongoing beers that contribute to our local waterways and conservationists (including the Tennessee Aquarium and Tennessee River Gorge Trust)

How do you decide on new beers to brew?

Nathan - New beers are especially fun to come up with. We really try to focus on the brew. Typically if we have a name first we like to cater to the name somewhat. If the beer comes first, we try to look at the market of trending beers or do something brand new and work within style guidelines to create something amazing! We also try to have beers on tap that reflect the weather. We often see that when its sunny and hot people like more light and easy drinking beers, whereas, when its cold or rainy outside it tends to be perfect weather to cuddle up to a nice dark malty beer

What are the biggest reasons for the continual growth of craft breweries?

Nathan - Breweries are continuing to grow due to the fact that people are open to trying new things and want to support local businesses now more than ever. Typically there are multiple breweries within each city these days, and all of them have a different atmosphere, style, and offer a wide variety of brews. So rather than drinking the same beer at 10 bars, you can now have over 100 different beers at 10 bars.

What are the biggest obstacles to continued craft beer growth?

Jake - Producing products like seltzers that are not craft and anyone can do. What separates breweries apart is making killer beers with unique and complex ingredients, not sugar and fruit flavors.

Nathan - Right now the biggest issue in the year of 2020 is getting more draft to the people. Can sales are the future for craft breweries and many people have streamlined this, however, with more people buying and purchasing more cans, supply lines can sometimes get pushed back. One of the biggest challenges to echo our owner is the amount of marketable low carb- low calorie options in the market. People are always going to be health conscious in a sense and the market flooded with many options are

What are the biggest problems you run into in producing beer?

Nathan - Some of the biggest problems we run into as far as producing beer depends on trends. Some seasonal trends can cause ordering issues due to the fact that everyone wants to use the same ingredients. For example, it's hard to contract certain hops or fruit adjuncts depending on the time of year, crop, harvest, and demand.

How do you reach beyond the hardcore beer drinkers and into the general public to sell your beer?

Jake - Producing a style for everyone We like to offer something for everyone.

Nathan - We have a fantastic location in Chattanooga, TN across from the UTC stadium. Not only do we have a great location, but we offer a kid friendly space, dog friendly patio, and full bbq food menu. We have a new can artist that has been making killer designs to help brand our beers in the public. We offer great deals on beer and we are one of the only breweries to

How did you first discover craft beer and what made you want to enter the business?

Jake - Local wateringhole only served beer, and rewarded you for the more you tried.

Nathan - I grew up drinking some pretty widespread beers. I remember when Fat Tire became distributed in my home state and falling in love. This really sparked my interest in drinking more and better craft beers. After that I really started exploring localized breweries and pubs to try to find a new beer or something to spark my interest. I vividly remember sitting at Pisgah Brewing Company in Black Mountain, NC and declaring that "I could totally make beer." My life was forever changed by a microbrewery.

How do you attempt to increase beer production while still staying true to both your brand and your unique styles?

Nathan - We increase production by constructing new recipes, and distributing to new locations. Our sales team is extremely well versed in selling beer and promoting our brand! We also try to involve the community as much as possible. We have even done brew days that are open to the public. We are extremely open to talking to people about beer and helping introduce them to new styles.

What's the style most fun to brew?

Nathan - The most fun style beer to brew is the one your most passionate about. I love brewing experimental beers or styles, if we have a benefit or collaboration beer, those are always the most fun to brew.

What beer would you brew if cost, production, and sales were no object?

Nathan - We really don't have any conflict with this question, we are pretty open to brewing anything. But that style and beer reflect what we would need to brew it. Right now nothing is stopping us from making any new beers.

Is there a popular beer you make that you just don't really like but everyone else loves?

Nathan - I love all my beers differently and I think they all have a unique enough profile. I agree there is something for everyone and every occasion. I have grown a little more and more

End of a long brew day, what are you drinking?

Nathan - Something cold, haha. My preferences change all the time and we produce around 16 different beers year round.

What are a few beers that other brewers are making that you really find impressive?

Nathan - I find the most impressive beers to me are the harder styles to produce or a phenomenal use of the ingredients

How do you feel the internet has changed the way the craft brewing industry operates?

Nathan - I think the internet has been an amazing resource for new techniques, brew styles, and new ideas that can easily help most brewer's day to day. Wifi and Bluetooth have been a major increase in monitoring daily functioning operations.

When coming out with a new brew, how much experimentation do you try to get in before you say it's ready for production?

Nathan - Depending on the beer and style, often we wing' it and brew it. For our more intensive beers we try to pilot brew 2x-6x times before running it on the production scale.

What style of beer is your bestseller and why do you think that is?

Nathan - We currently have 2 best sellers, one being our Moon Pie Stout, due to the fact that we are using locally sourced Moonpies and appeal to the masses with the representation. Our other best seller is a German style Pilsner (Naked Light 5.0%) this is a crystal clear lager and super refreshing, crisp light finish. We try our hardest to convert macro beer fans over to our Naked Light

Does glassware really make a difference?

Nathan - I think that 80% of styles can be consumed out of similar glasses. I agree that IPA glasses, goblets, and shaker pints are the best go-to for almost all beers.

What's the real difference between a Porter and a Stout?

Nathan - You tell me??? Most brewers claim one or the other for their beers, and people will drink accordingly. Depending on your beer knowledge it comes down to minimal differences, but overall the origin of the styles vary but most differences in brewing get blurred.

How important is IBU when it comes to picking out a beer? Do customers need to pay attention to it?

Nathan - IBUs are very important to consumers. Typically your Average Joe won't care about IBUs, however, your hopheads definitely care. If your bartenders are helping new craft drinkers decide what beer to drink it can also be super beneficial in helping them decide, which can mean more beer sales.

NOVEL BREWING COMPANY

6510 San Pablo Avenue
Oakland, CA 94608

Teresa Tamburello
Co-owner and Operations Manager

Typically, how much beer do you guys make in a year?

Right below 500 bbls

How much beer do you personally consume on an average workday?

Probably about a pint -- split over many sips / tastes

What's your favorite food to eat with beer and why?

Pizza or anything salty -- the beer cleanses the palette

When you first opened the brewery, what was the biggest obstacle? What advice would you give someone thinking about opening a brewery to avoid some pitfalls you experienced?

We downsized the brew house from 7 to 3.5 bbl, due to construction costs going up. I would never advise anyone to start a brewery with less than a 7 bbl system.

Does glassware really make a difference?

Yes

End of a long brew day, what are you drinking?

A light lager.

NEXUS BREWERY

4730 Pan American Fwy NE Ste D
Albuquerque, NM 87109

Ken Carson, Jr.
Owner

Typically, how much beer do you guys make in a year?

About 700 to 800 barrels

How much beer do you personally consume on an average workday?

None at work. 2 to 3 beers 3 times weekly

What's your favorite food to eat with beer and why?

Our food, fried catfish and collard greens or in general soul food

About how much does it cost to open a brewery?

Half million

What are today's worst beer trends?

I think that the younger generation is not as into beer as the 30 and above

When you first opened the brewery, what was the biggest obstacle? What advice would you give someone thinking about opening a brewery to avoid some pitfalls you experienced?

Capital was a big obstacle and getting to profitability. Anticipate Plan A, then if that does not work go to B, then C and you better have a D. Nothing works like you expect be thrifty on how you spend because what you plan to spend even with good research will not be enough. Unless you have done this before.

How do you decide on new beers to brew?

I let the brewers do their thing with some input

How did you first discover craft beer and what made you want to enter the business?

I was a banker for 35 years. I found you could make your own beer before it was fashionable. Every time I left town I would find the local brewery.

What beer would you brew if cost, production, and sales were no object?

High alcohol scotch ale at 16%

Does glassware really make a difference?

Yes, but we have not focused on that.

What beer is your brewery best known for and why?

Imperial Cream

End of a long brew day, what are you drinking?

Scotch Ale

NEWPORT CRAFT BREWING AND DISTILLING

293 JT Connell Hwy
Newport, RI 02840

Brendan O'Donnell
CEO

Typically, how much beer do you guys make in a year?

In 2019 we produced 4,500 BBL of beer. 2020 we are projecting around 7,500 BBLs. We are also about to acquire a very strong brewery out of NYC.

How much beer do you personally consume on an average workday?

I will taste different beers for reference and quality control, but during the week usually not more than one.

What's your favorite food to eat with beer and why?

Pizza. For me, it goes with any beer and a greasy, cheesy pizza with a nice cold beer is the perfect combo.

About how much does it cost to open a brewery?

It depends on several factors. Are you buying the land? Where are you opening it geographically? How big are you trying to be? The barrier to entry of the last couple of years has become much less with new models without distribution and smaller equipment, it really depends on what you are trying to accomplish. I would say at the minimum you are looking at $500,000. Depends how much debt you are taking on, the current environment is very lucrative for rates and borrowing.

What are today's worst beer trends?

Haha, hmm. I love the creativity In the industry and everyone pushing the boundaries, but I personally am not a fan of low calorie IPAs. I think it's more of a marketing push than anything else and if you are drinking an IPA, you should not be worrying about the calories, you should be worrying about the taste.

When you first opened the brewery, what was the biggest obstacle?

It was a different circumstance for us because we bought into the Brewery and eventually became 100% owners. The biggest obstacle for us was changing the perception of what the brewery use to be as we were revamping it. What advice would you give someone thinking about opening a brewery to avoid some pitfalls you experienced? Don't be afraid to take chances, but don't chase trends and know your customer. It may be the hot thing to make a brut IPA, but your customer may not want that, so don't waste time, resources, and money on chasing trends that your customer may not want.

How do you decide on new beers to brew?

We interact a lot with our customers and are constantly testing. We try to have a portfolio that covers a range of styles, but for new beers it depends on how large of a release we are doing. If it's a small barrel program release we will do something more nitch like a farmhouse, imperial stout etc. If it's a beer that we are trying to do year round or a larger release, we usually will test several beers for up to six months and make sure we build up a lot of demand so that when we release it we are able to distribute it on a larger scale.

How did you first discover craft beer and what made you want to enter the business?

When I did a semester in Prague, Czech Republic in 2007. Most restaurants brewed their own beers and they were so fresh, I never knew beer could taste like that. Then I went to the Pilsner Urquell facility and I was hooked.

What beer would you brew if cost, production, and sales were no object?

Helles Lagers. Doesn't make sense for us to do on a large scale, but I love them.

Does glassware really make a difference?

Yes.

What beer is your brewery best known for and why?

Our Rhode Trip New England IPA. It's very approachable and we use the best hops available that craft beer drinkers seek out. It's a very balanced easy drinking beer anytime of the year and also has a great name and branding.

End of a long brew day, what are you drinking?

Right now our Braven Bright Lights Pale Ale.

NORTH FORK BREWING COMPANY

24 E 2nd St Ste A
Riverhead, NY 11901

Michelle Demetillo
Hospitality + Community Manager

What's your favorite food to eat with beer and why?

There is something to me about eating sushi with beer, especially if it contains ginger or has a bitterness to complement the umami flavors found in sushi. I love trying ethnic cuisines with beer and experimenting with the complex flavors that are found in both the food and beer. It can totally change your perception of the two, depending on what cuisines and styles you're pairing together.

What are the biggest reasons for the continual growth of craft breweries?

I think there is a large number of breweries that are becoming community hubs. Society is becoming more open-minded and receptive about craft beer as it continues to grow. As beer education and awareness is on the rise, I believe people can more easily find a style that fits their preferences. Palates are changing, and people want more than the old party staples in the cooler. They are also recognizing that a craft brewery is not just another bar in their neighborhood. You can bring your dog and kids to the brewery, and it's pretty much acceptable. You can bring your grandparents to the brewery and they may wind up enjoying themselves. You can gather with your book club or running group. You can celebrate your engagement at a brewery; you can even get engaged there. You can celebrate your parents' wedding anniversary there, or a memorial to a loved one at a brewery. These are spaces to celebrate and make memories, and not just a space to produce and consume alcohol.

How do you feel the internet has changed the way the craft brewing industry operates?

Social media 100% sells our business and the brand. Without the internet and social media platforms, I don't think many breweries would have the sales, customer base, ease of recognition, and traffic that they do. Social media allows us to follow trends and know what beer fans want. Also, it pushes the fact that branding and marketing are so incredibly important, not only in this industry but in every industry. While word of mouth has always been and is still effective, internet reviews and effective marketing can travel so much further these days. I don't think we'd have as many successful breweries today if it weren't for the internet.

How important is IBU when it comes to picking out a beer? Do customers need to pay attention to it?

As someone who has a "the more bitter the better" mentality, IBU is certainly something that I look for. I do try and educate patrons that come into the brewery as well. When it may be an individual who is not a fan of bitterness, I let them know that IBU is a measurement that they can look at. However, carbonation and certain adjuncts do add to or subtract from perceived bitterness, which everyone should be aware of. However, I do think it is a good gauge for people who know what they enjoy and in educating new beer fans.

NEW ENGLAND BREWING CO.

175 Amity Rd
Woodbridge, CT 06525

Marty Juliano
Director of Business Development

Typically, how much beer do you guys produce in an average year?

18,000 Bbls

What's your favorite food to eat with beer and why?

Pizza, Burgers, Steak...it all depends on the beer style you want to pair with

About how much money does it cost to open a brewery?

This depends on what size brewery you open...ranges from $50,000 to millions

What are today's worst beer trends?

Brand loyalty as peoples shopping choices are what's new and what's next.

In the past few years we have seen a massive surge in the popularity of Hazy IPA's and Sours, what do you believe the next popular beer style will be?

Lagers / Pilsners

What beers are you best known for and why?

Sea Hag IPA, Fuzzy Baby Ducks IPA, G-Bot (Ghandi Bot pre name change) and Imperial Stout Trooper. The beers are very consistent and Our Artwork on the cans along with the names resonate with consumers.

What sets your brewery apart from most others?

Quality and Consistency along with the culture.

How do you decide on new beers to brew?

Our brewers have a pilot brew system to develop recipes on and consumer response on those beers help us make the decision to brew a larger batch and release it.

How did you first discover craft beer and what made you want to enter the business?

Sierra Nevada Pale Ale was the entrance to craft for me. As for getting into the business, I started part time at a liquor store in high school and it morphed from there after college.

How do you attempt to increase beer production while still staying true to both your brand and your unique styles?

By not growing too fast at once. Slow manageable growth year after year is sustainable and allows for creativity while focusing on Sea Hag our flagship beer.

End of a long brew day, what are you drinking?

Pilsner or Helles Lager

What are a few beers that other brewers are making that you really find impressive?

Anything from Sierra Nevada as they are always awesome beers. Allagash White and any of their sours. They are on the same level as Sierra on quality and consistency

What style of beer is your bestseller and why do you think that is?

IPA's are the best sellers and that is due to customer demand

Does glassware really make a difference?

Absolutely yes it does!

NECK OF THE WOODS BREWING

614 Lambs Road, Suite 7
Pitman, NJ 08071

Frank Price
Owner and Brewer

Typically, how much beer do you guys make in a year?

We have only been opened for 1 year now. I think we brewed in the neighborhood of 11K gallons of beer or 350 barrels of beer.

How much beer do you personally consume on an average workday?

It really depends on the week but on average less than 1

What's your favorite food to eat with beer and why?

Pretzels—hard nugget size. The salt is a palate cleanser and really allows the flavors of the beer to shine!

About how much does it cost to open a brewery?

3x what you initially think it will. For us we need at least 1/2 mil to get started.

What are today's worst beer trends?

Trends themselves. We try to be our own. I despise looking at social media and following what ever other brewery is doing. Be yourself, brew beer that you like to drink. Brew beer that will also sell.

When you first opened the brewery, what was the biggest obstacle? What advice would you give someone thinking about opening a brewery to avoid some pitfalls you experienced?

The biggest obstacle was lack of experience in this field. Hire a reputable consultant Day 0 when you planning a brewery and you will save yourself $ and headaches in the long run.

How do you decide on new beers to brew?

Follow our sales trends. If sours are killing it, then brew another fruited one. If DIPA's are popular, then brew another one. As far as flavors and hop selection, its trial and error—but don't take big risks.

How did you first discover craft beer and what made you want to enter the business?

I discovered craft from my brother in law. Hated IPA's at first but gradually learned to love them. We have a passion for craft and when the consumers respond in a positive way it makes you want to craft some more.

What beer would you brew if cost, production, and sales were no object?

Barrel aged beers every day. Sourcing and storing barrels can be expensive and difficult to do from a space perspective. I'd love to see a warehouse full of barrel aged every kind of beer!

Does glassware really make a difference?

Absolutely. There is definitely a science behind it for sure. Plus if it looks cool your brain will perceive the beer as tasting better.

What beer is your brewery best known for and why?

Stay in the car Frank IPA. It's just a cool name and people read it and laugh.

End of a long brew day, what are you drinking?

Nothing quenches the thirst of a hot day on the brewdeck like a cold refreshing juicy IPA.

NEW MADISON BREWING

3463 Shun Pike Rd
Madison, IN 47250

Nick Privette
Head Brewer

How much beer do you personally consume on an average workday?

On a brew day, none. On a tap room day, a few.

What's your favorite food to eat with beer and why?

Beer is food so more beer.

What are today's worst beer trends?

Milkshake and slushy beers. They taste horrible but people like the hunt. I
don't consider the spritzers as beer.

In the past few years we have seen a massive surge in the popularity of Hazy IPA's and Sours, what do you believe the next popular beer style will be?

Cheap craft beer of any standard style.

When you first opened the brewery, what was the biggest obstacle? What advice would you give someone thinking about opening a brewery to avoid some of the pitfalls you experienced?

Work with your state and local government officials early in the process. Don't assume anything.

What beers are you best known for and why?

Probably our Raspberry Wheat. It's dry and easy drinking; people are pleasantly surprised it isn't sweet.

How do you decide on new beers to brew?

Customer input and or whatever sounds like fun at the time.

What are the biggest obstacles to continued craft beer growth?

The market is already saturated. The economy will not support it moving forward.

What are the biggest problems you run into in producing beer?

Finding the time to do it as we work separate day jobs.

How do you reach beyond the hardcore beer drinkers and into the general public to sell your beer?

We don't feel the need to cater to only the hardcore. We cater to beer drinkers. We sell a variety of styles.

What's the style most fun to brew?

Sours

What beer would you brew if cost, production, and sales were no object?

Big Belgian beers and sours

End of a long brew day, what are you drinking?

Cold water

What are a few beers that other brewers are making that you really find impressive?

New Glarus's Wisconsin Red is one of the best beers I've had and probably the best American brewed beer I've had. Jai Alai by Cigar City is about the perfect IPA for me; it's the only one I repeatedly purchase. Miller High Life is still an excellent beer, although a macro.

When coming out with a new brew, how much experimentation do you try to get in before you say it's ready for production?

Typically once or twice on our pilot system with customer input.

What's the real difference between a Porter and a Stout?

Stout has roasted barley. Black to chocolate ratio to a lesser extent.

How important is IBU when it comes to picking out a beer? Do customers need to pay attention to it?

It's important to IPA drinkers who are looking for a bitter or less bitter IPA, but other styles should already be balanced.

NEW REALM BREWING

550 Somerset Ter NE Unit 101
Atlanta, GA 30306

Mitch Steele
Brewmaster, COO and Co-Founder

Typically, how much beer do you guys make in a year?

We only have two years' history, so It's hard to say. The first year we did
5-6000 bbls and last year we did closer to 12,000 bbls. That includes two
locations with full service restaurants, which sells a large proportion of
our beer.

How much beer do you personally consume on an average workday?

Very little. I've been in this business a long time, and as I've gotten older
my daily beer consumption has reduced to maybe just a couple of pints a

week. I do taste beer frequently during the week, but that's different, and accounts for maybe 8-10 oz of beer per session.

What's your favorite food to eat with beer and why?

Artisanal cheese is my favorite food to pair with beer. A sharp, tangy, salty cheese just matches up perfectly with malty sweetness and hop flavor and bitterness. I really enjoy trying to find that perfect combination.

About how much does it cost to open a brewery?

A lot more than you think it will. I've heard many brewers say to expect double your initial budget and 6 months longer than your initial time line. I think that holds true in many cases. There are so many unpredictable things that will happen that raise the costs and slow down the process. Actual cost depends on the size. A small nano you can probably get away with a few hundred thousand dollars, but once you start adding tap rooms or a restaurant, you're going to go much higher.

What are today's worst beer trends?

The one that is toughest for me is the continued loss of relevance of the beer styles that got us here. Pale Ales, Barley Wines, Amber Ales are all struggling in today's craft beer scene. And that's a shame. These are the styles that craft beer was built on. And they are still tasty.

When you first opened the brewery, what was the biggest obstacle? What advice would you give someone thinking about opening a brewery to avoid some pitfalls you experienced?

Dealing with things that are out of your control, like permit timing, and other government approvals. Realize that you are at their mercy when it comes to getting this stuff completed, which is why you need to pad your timeline. If you don't like project management, you aren't going to enjoy the process of opening a brewery.

How do you decide on new beers to brew?

Lots of different ways. We have a creative team that provides suggestions and ideas, we pay attention to the latest innovation in the industry, and we listen to our guests and customers. New hop varieties are coming out all the time-and these fuel the creative process of recipe formulation. All of these help drive any decision to brew something new. And every once in a while, we will brew something just because we like the style, or we want to learn more about brewing it.

How did you first discover craft beer and what made you want to enter the business?

My first craft beer was Anchor Steam Beer and that got me excited about what malts can do to the flavor and color of a beer. It so was so different than most the beers I had tried up to that point. A college trip to Sierra Nevada Brewing Co. is what sold me on craft beer and made me want to brew professionally.

What beer would you brew if cost, production, and sales were no object?

I would brew historical beers that no longer exist as a style, or continue to brew massively hoppy IPAs.

Does glassware really make a difference?

It sure does! The aromatics of a beer manifest themselves in many different ways, depending in part on the shape of the glass. The shaker pint glass is one of the worst glasses for beer, but a tulip shaped glass helps concentrate and release the aromatics in a beer, and works well as a multipurpose glass.

What beer is your brewery best known for and why?

Well our Euphonia Pilsner has won the most awards-it's a classic German hoppy Pilsner. But our best selling beer is Hazy Like A Fox New England style IPA. It's very drinkable and loaded with juicy flavor. I'm known as an IPA brewer so I think people pay a little more attention to our IPAs than other styles we brew

End of a long brew day, what are you drinking?

A lot of water, then either a Euphonia Pilsner or our Hoplandia IPA-a "classic" west coast IPA dry hopped with Centennial and Simcoe.

OLD COAST ALES

300 Anastasia Blvd Ste C
Saint Augustine, FL 32080

Matthew Hooker

Typically, how much beer do you guys make in a year?

370 bbls

How much beer do you personally consume on an average workday?

About 2 or 3 pints - in tastes & short pours

What's your favorite food to eat with beer and why?

Tacos - because we have a really good taco place next door.

About how much does it cost to open a brewery?

Much more than anticipated. Ours is a 7 bbl system. Today you could bootstrap that size for 200k +-

What are today's worst beer trends?

LoCal & hard seltzer

When you first opened the brewery, what was the biggest obstacle?

For us it was our lease/landlord - Delays on the building that were out of our control cost mucho.

What advice would you give someone thinking about opening a brewery to avoid some pitfalls you experienced?

For advice, maybe a brewery specific law firm to help navigate the business side. Would be money well spent unless you have a background in business (mba), etc. And do not underestimate the need for fermentation & cold room capacity. These are the 2 main "bottlenecks". Plan ahead for future needs, not just start up.

How do you decide on new beers to brew?

There are 2 of us as owners. We have similar tastes and keep up with breweries that we respect. When we try something that has a "wow" factor, it does have an influence in what we do.

How did you first discover craft beer and what made you want to enter the business?

Probably Sierra Nevada & Sam Adams were early influencers. As homebrewers, our beers were really good and we said: "I wonder if we could make a living brewing beer" & a book "Brewery Operations Manual" by Tom hennessy

What beer would you brew if cost, production, and sales were no object?

Probably a true foeder/barrel aged sour.

Does glassware really make a difference?

We say yes! Enjoyment of craft beer includes sight, aroma, & taste.

What beer is your brewery best known for and why?

Empirical IPA It has been our flagship beer since opening.

End of a long brew day, what are you drinking?

A nice refreshing hazy IPA

OLD HARBOR BREWERY

1 M Riveria Ferrer
Guiynavo, PR 00968

William J Cruz

Typically, how much beer do you guys make in a year?

3,000 to 4,000 Bbl

2. How much beer do you personally consume on an average workday?

None, 0.

What's your favorite food to eat with beer and why?

Meat, Burger, etc.

About how much does it cost to open a brewery?

With Kegs, bottling, Bar and accounting department > $1,000,000.00

What are today's worst beer trends?

Sour

When you first opened the brewery, what was the biggest obstacle? What advice would you give someone thinking about opening a brewery to avoid some pitfalls you experienced?

Permits, permits, money.

How do you decide on new beers to brew?

Committee consultation.

How did you first discover craft beer and what made you want to enter the business?

It's a Fun business.

What beer would you brew if cost, production, and sales were no object?

Pilsner, Pale Ale.

Does glassware really make a difference?

YES, A Big difference. Must be in a clear glass.

What beer is your brewery best known for and why?

Pilsner, Melon flavor, Helles. Because the warm weather.

End of a long brew day, what are you drinking?

Old Harbor Brewery ; Santo Viejo - Pilsner. Awarded in a number of competitions in USA.

OVERSHORES BREWING CO.

250 Bradley St
East Haven, CT 06512

Christian Amport

Typically, how much beer do you guys make in a year?

Most production breweries are highly variable. Most small breweries are still growing and there is no such thing as a "typical" year unless you're the type of place that has been around for 20 years and has topped out and found a routine, stable market (which are not common nowadays). Pubs can be more consistent in their year-over-year production numbers because they have a better idea of how much beer they themselves can go through.

Generally the amount of beer you make is not a function of production capacity. It's a function of how much beer you can sell/get people to buy.

Capacity is easy to add. Sales is what is what drives growth. If you can't turn over what you make, you can't grow.

How much beer do you personally consume on an average workday?

I personally rarely have a full beer at work. I'll taste things here and there. Every once in a while I'll have a beer but it's not the norm for me. I frankly have too much I need to do in a day and having a beer during work often derails productivity for the sake of conversation. I save it for after work.

What's your favorite food to eat with beer and why?

Buffalo wings. Something about the maltiness of a cold beer cuts through the heat and is so satisfying.

About how much does it cost to open a brewery?

"A brewery" can be a 1 bbl open top pot system on a turkey fryer in a commercially leased garage or it can be a 20 million dollar facility funded by private equity investors and everything in between. It depends on what you're doing and where. For a purpose built commercial system in either a production facility that's big enough to support 3-5 full time employees, or in a restaurant/pub with a kitchen and enough tables to pay for the employees needed to run a restaurant, count on at a minimum a million dollars and more is better.

What are today's worst beer trends?

Collecting, hype and lies. People are too easily manipulated by breweries willing to lie to them regarding uniqueness and scarcity (or lack thereof) and are too eager to try to impress strangers by standing in line for hours or by letting social media be the driving factor in building a collection of beers in your basement that will just gather dust.

When you first opened the brewery, what was the biggest obstacle? What advice would you give someone thinking about opening a brewery to avoid some pitfalls you experienced?

Money. Everything costs way more than you think and getting to the point where you're getting money back takes much longer than you think.

How do you decide on new beers to brew?

What's happening in the market. It sounds cynical and trend chasing but the reality is that a brewery is a business. It's not just a big homebrew system where you make what you like and people buy it and it pays for your hobby. That mentality is why breweries lose relevance in the market and go out of business or fail to grow. The bigger a brewery gets, the more pressure there is to stay on trend because the market changes so fast, beers lose relevance so fast, people's interest changes so fast, that in order to maintain turnover of your production, you have to stay on trend. There's a wide world of beers out there that are wonderful but are not commercially viable. A ton of people got into the business specifically because they started homebrewing stuff that was hard to find or out of fashion. The dream of starting a brewery doing all English cask ales or Belgian style beers is not unique. Those styles, while delicious if done well, have very little scalability. The Belgian white trend 7 years ago was evidence of this. There's not a ton of demand out there for Belgian whites but for a second it was hot because Blue Moon and Allagash had found a niche. Turned out not to be a big niche. People order and purchase IPAs and lagers one after another. That's there the commercial volume is. We can all fill out a portfolio of different things to offer but when you look at volume, it's IPAs and lagers and will be for a while. Everything else is window dressing for variety's sake. IPAs and lagers pay the bills. The rest just fills tanks.

How did you first discover craft beer and what made you want to enter the business?

Living in Vermont in the early 2000's I discovered Magic Hat and others and got into what Unibroue was doing with Belgian styles in Quebec. I wanted to bring what Unibroue, Allagash and Ommegang were doing to my home of Connecticut. I was looking to change careers by my late 20's and decided to make the shift.

What beer would you brew if cost, production, and sales were no object?

Belgians. I still do but it doesn't pay the bills sadly. It's a passion project at this point.

Does glassware really make a difference?

Absolutely. Presentation, tactile experience and bouquet are all part of the experience.

What beer is your brewery best known for and why?

Hard to say. We operate now as a cooperative brewing space and are home to 12 different brands, mine (Overshores) only being one of them.

End of a long brew day, what are you drinking?

8 year rum on the rocks. When you're around beer all day long, every day, it's nice to have something else at the end of the day.

ON TOUR BREWING CO.

1725 W Hubbard St
Chicago, IL 60622

Mark Legenza

Typically, how much beer do you guys make in a year?

1,000 bbls

How much beer do you personally consume on an average workday?

None. I don't drink during the work day

What's your favorite food to eat with beer and why?

Pizza. I'm a born and raised Chicagoan!

About how much does it cost to open a brewery?

$1,000,000

What are today's worst beer trends?

Rating beers online based on one sip out of a shared taster

When you first opened the brewery, what was the biggest obstacle? What advice would you give someone thinking about opening a brewery to avoid some pitfalls you experienced?

There are a lot of obstacles to open a brewery. My advice would be if you love problem solving this is the business for you. If you don't, go work for someone else and you'll be happier.

How do you decide on new beers to brew?

At On Tour, we try to span the full spectrum of beer. We brew based on what we need to keep our menu diverse and fresh. New beers are often inspired by traveling or new experiences including food, nature, etc. Inspiration can be found anywhere if you're open to find it.

How did you first discover craft beer and what made you want to enter the business?

In my late teens I traveled the country following bands. There were a lot of people selling single bottles of beer to drink on the way into the show. A lot of people were traveling the country as well so they brought beer from their hometowns. I was exposed to a lot of early craft beer and imports in the late 90's that shaped my love for a full flavor beverage. I've always been a hard worker and entrepreneurial. Once I grew a love for homebrewing my hobby and professional experience overlapped and felt right.

What beer would you brew if cost, production, and sales were no object?

Expanding our barrel aged sour program would be my first choice.

Does glassware really make a difference?

Personally I don't believe it does make a difference. However, I do have all the glassware at our brewery and my home. I feel glassware adds to the experience and another way to enjoy a beer. But under a blind taste test I don't feel the majority of consumers could tell the difference.

What beer is your brewery best known for and why?

Lightning Will Pilsner has been on our menu from day one. It's a solid pilsner that has won some awards and the first beer people think of when they hear On Tour Brewing Co.

12. End of a long brew day, what are you drinking?

5.5% IPA or Pale Ale

OPPOSITION BREWING COMPANY

545 Rossanley Dr Ste 106
Medford, OR 97501

Nick Ellis
Founder & CEO

Typically, how much beer do you guys produce in an average year?

It varies but around 200bbls

How much beer do you personally consume on an average workday?

LOL... um... let's go with 24oz. ;-p (not at work of course... afterwards)

What's your favorite food to eat with beer and why?

Nothing specific really... except NOT sweets. outside of a stout, perhaps, i
don't like how beer pairs with desserts/candy.

About how much money does it cost to open a brewery?

Depends entirely on what kind of brewery you're looking to open.

What are today's worst beer trends?

I'm not sure there's any really "bad" trends right now that i'm aware of. i think the hazy ipa thing has sort of played itself out but that's normal for something to flood the market and then peter out eventually.

In the past few years we have seen a massive surge in the popularity of Hazy IPA's and Sours, what do you believe the next popular beer style will be?

Really hard to say. all depends on consumer demand. all we can do is make new and innovative beers and see what becomes popular! for us, as we enter the summer months, fruited wheats are always really popular so we'll start producing a lot of those.

When you first opened the brewery, what was the biggest obstacle? What advice would you give someone thinking about opening a brewery to avoid some of the pitfalls you experienced?

City permitting costs and red tape. be prepared to deal with a municipality that isn't particularly business friendly.

What beers are you best known for and why?

We make a northwest pale ale (think balanced ipa) that's our biggest seller.

What sets your brewery apart from most others?

We don't deal in pretense. we're a bare bones brewery with a super down to earth personality. no frills here!

How do you decide on new beers to brew?

We brew what we like to drink and we're willing to try anything as long as it meets that criteria.

What are the biggest reasons for the continual growth of craft breweries?

I don't know that there is going to be continual growth of the craft brewery scene. Even before covid hit the industry was seeing market contraction.

What are the biggest obstacles to continued craft beer growth?

Market saturation. We'll see continued market contraction, I believe, for a while.

What are the biggest problems you run into in producing beer?

Often it's hop supply. The mega breweries contract for such huge volumes of hops, for the popular varieties, it often leaves us small guys out of luck.

How do you reach beyond the hardcore beer drinkers and into the general public to sell your beer?

Offer a wide selection of beer profiles. not everyone is a mega hop head or a light beer drinker. You need a wide variety.

How did you first discover craft beer and what made you want to enter the business?

It was just a natural progression into drinking craft beer... which I think is pretty natural for most beer drinkers. I got into the business because I got laid off from my corporate job and needed something to do!

How do you attempt to increase beer production while still staying true to both your brand and your unique styles?

Slowly. Organically. Forced growth generally results in risky business. We have no investors and no bank loans. All growth has been revenue driven.

What's the style most fun to brew?

I really love flanders style sours. They're tremendously hard and time intensive to produce, but they're also super fun.

What beer would you brew if cost, production, and sales were no object?

Flanders?

Is there a popular beer you make that you just don't really like but everyone else loves?

We make a super popular cream ale. It's our attempt at appealing to the light beer drinker. It's good, but just not my jam. We brew and sell a lot of it though!

End of a long brew day, what are you drinking?

If we're talking my own beer, it would be our NWPA. If we're talking someone else's, Goodlife Descender IPA

What are a few beers that other brewers are making that you really find impressive?

Cascade brewing and Russian River have both really nailed the whole sour beer thing. Some of my fav specialty beers. Such skill. So impressive.

How do you feel the internet has changed the way the craft brewing industry operates?

Social media is where it is right now. It's made marketing virtually free for breweries and have amazing reach. For small guys like us it's a godsend.

When coming out with a new brew, how much experimentation do you try to get in before you say it's ready for production?

None. we're on a 1.5bbl system. i just develop a recipe and we brew it. if it's not super delicious and/or just doesn't sell, we just don't brew it again.

What style of beer is your bestseller and why do you think that is?

Our NWPA. it's a balanced IPA that doesn't taste like your chewing on a hop cone.

Does glassware really make a difference?

Absolutely. it's all about aroma. smell is the majority of taste... proper glassware can really bring out the intended flavor of a beer.

What's the real difference between a Porter and a Stout?

In my opinion a porter is sweeter and softer in profile than a stout. We don't care much for porters but love stouts... which is why we only brew stouts.

How important is IBU when it comes to picking out a beer? Do customers need to pay attention to it?

For me it matters only in that I know I don't care for huge IBU beers. In general though, folks who like ipa's are always interested in those higher IBU numbers. I think customers would be better served though if they simply tasted a beer without consideration to the IBU number and make a decision that way rather than just going for whatever is has the highest or lowest rating.

353

OLD STOVE BREWING COMPANY

1901 Western Ave
Seattle, WA 98101

Brian Stan

Typically, how much beer do you guys produce in an average year?

2019 = 2,100 Barrels

How much beer do you personally consume on an average workday?

2 pints

What's your favorite food to eat with beer and why?

Varies, depending on type of beer

About how much money does it cost to open a brewery?

A lot more than we planned!

What are today's worst beer trends?

COVID-19

In the past few years we have seen a massive surge in the popularity of Hazy IPA's and Sours, what do you believe the next popular beer style will be?

Lagers

When you first opened the brewery, what was the biggest obstacle? What advice would you give someone thinking about opening a brewery to avoid some of the pitfalls you experienced?

Pad your estimates

What beers are you best known for and why?

Rotating IPA's, Pastry Stouts, etc.

What sets your brewery apart from most others?

Quality, location, and vibe

How do you decide on new beers to brew?

Team decision

What are the biggest reasons for the continual growth of craft breweries?

Good beer

What are the biggest obstacles to continued craft beer growth?

COVID-19

What are the biggest problems you run into in producing beer?

Capacity

How do you reach beyond the hardcore beer drinkers and into the general public to sell your beer?

Packaging

How did you first discover craft beer and what made you want to enter the business?

In PNW, at a restaurant

How do you attempt to increase beer production while still staying true to both your brand and your unique styles?

Same

What's the style most fun to brew?

Collabs

What beer would you brew if cost, production, and sales were no object?

6+lbs/BBL IPA

Is there a popular beer you make that you just don't really like but everyone else loves?

Pepper Beer

End of a long brew day, what are you drinking?

Pilsner

What are a few beers that other brewers are making that you really find impressive?

Tons

How do you feel the internet has changed the way the craft brewing industry operates?

For the better

When coming out with a new brew, how much experimentation do you try to get in before you say it's ready for production?

Depends on the beer. Some

What style of beer is your bestseller and why do you think that is?

IPA

Does glassware really make a difference?

Yes

What's the real difference between a Porter and a Stout?

Stout stronger

How important is IBU when it comes to picking out a beer? Do customers need to pay attention to it?

Occasionally

PARADISE BREWING / PARADISE BREWING SUPPLIES

7766 Beechmont Ave
Cincinnati, OH 45255

Jeff Graff

Typically, how much beer do you guys make in a year?

270 BBLs annually

How much beer do you personally consume on an average workday?

We do not drink everyday. We couldn't get any work done.

What's your favorite food to eat with beer and why?

We provide (or did provide prior to Covid) peanut butter pretzel pieces.
That works.

About how much does it cost to open a brewery?

We opened "organically". We started making 10 gallon batches. 3 years ago, we took on investors and now are a 5 BBL brewhouse.

What are today's worst beer trends?

I'm not a big fan of seltzers and sours.

When you first opened the brewery, what was the biggest obstacle? What advice would you give someone thinking about opening a brewery to avoid some pitfalls you experienced?

Biggest obstacle to me was cash flow. Keeping things moving when trends slow.

How do you decide on new beers to brew?

New beers and keeping it "fresh" is quite difficult. Normally, our recipe selection is seasonal. People's tastes change throughout the year.

How did you first discover craft beer and what made you want to enter the business?

I was working 2 jobs and could see 1 of the 2 declining and Brewing sky-rocketing upward. It was a no-brainer.

What beer would you brew if cost, production, and sales were no object?

More barrel aged beers.

Does glassware really make a difference?

Glassware, to me, makes minimal difference.

What beer is your brewery best known for and why?

Our customers have favorites that they look forward to throughout the season. Not one particular one.

End of a long brew day, what are you drinking?

Anything HOPPY.

Which hop varieties do you find yourself using most often and why?

I love Columbus. Others are: Simcoe, Mosaic, Citra and Cascade.

What was the first beer you ever brewed and how did it taste?

My first beer was a Killian's Irish Red clone and it hooked me. I couldn't replicate it until very later in my brewing career.

PROSPERITY BREWERS

4160 NW 1st Ave #20
Boca Raton, FL. 33431

Dominick Peri
Founder and CEO

Typically, how much beer do you guys make in a year?

400BBL

How much beer do you personally consume on an average workday?

3-4 pints

What's your favorite food to eat with beer and why?

Pizza

About how much does it cost to open a brewery?

10-15% more than u budget

What are today's worst beer trends?

Milkshake iPa's & pastry stouts

When you first opened the brewery, what was the biggest obstacle? What advice would you give someone thinking about opening a brewery to avoid some pitfalls you experienced?

The municipality's zoning and permitting. Either find a city that is brewery friendly or hire a local attorney to fight with city hall so you can stay positive and move the project forward.

How do you decide on new beers to brew?

Talk through it with the brew team monthly

How did you first discover craft beer and what made you want to enter the business?

Nantucket Cisco Brewers.... research it yourself, no words can explain it properly.

What beer would you brew if cost, production, and sales were no object?

Triple

Does glassware really make a difference?

Yes for both presentation and for controlling abv consumption

What beer is your brewery best known for and why?

Clutchplate IPA 6.9% abv dryhopped with Columbus. & Mosaic

End of a long brew day, what are you drinking?

Intra-KÖLSCH-Tal (kölsch l-style blonde ale)

Which hop varieties do you find yourself using most often and why?

Citra Mosaic cascade galaxy

What was the first beer you ever brewed and how did it taste?

Double dry hopped pale ale.... 1lb per gallon hops.... amazing!!

PESKY PELICAN BREWPUB

923 72nd St N
Saint Petersburg, FL 33710

Dan Pemberton

Typically, how much beer do you guys produce in an average year?

30 BBL

How much beer do you personally consume on an average workday?

During work, 0 After work 4-6

What's your favorite food to eat with beer and why?

Chicken Wings They just seem to go together

About how much money does it cost to open a brewery?

I bought a restaurant and started the brewery from there. I did not spend a lot as I still use my homebrew gear.

What are today's worst beer trends?

Kids Cereal flavors in beer

In the past few years we have seen a massive surge in the popularity of Hazy IPA's and Sours, what do you believe the next popular beer style will be?

I really don't know but it would be great if the masses would start enjoying flavors from some original styles like Ambers and stouts

When you first opened the brewery, what was the biggest obstacle? What advice would you give someone thinking about opening a brewery to avoid some of the pitfalls you experienced?

Don't own a restaurant. This is the hardest part of what I do.

What beers are you best known for and why?

Raspberry Wheat. It appeals to almost everyone.

What sets your brewery apart from most others?

Our food, and the fact we only brew 20 gallon batches

How do you decide on new beers to brew?

Seasonal

What are the biggest reasons for the continual growth of craft breweries?

People are finally realizing that beer should have flavor, not just fizz

What are the biggest obstacles to continued craft beer growth?

The three tier system and government regulation

What are the biggest problems you run into in producing beer?

Space

How do you reach beyond the hardcore beer drinkers and into the general public to sell your beer?

Our promotions always include food

How did you first discover craft beer and what made you want to enter the business?

I was in Colorado many years ago and had a Fat tire. I learned how to brew and the hobby became an obsession. Here we are today.

How do you attempt to increase beer production while still staying true to both your brand and your unique styles?

Brew more often lol

What's the style most fun to brew?

I have been having fun with many styles and Kveik yeast

What beer would you brew if cost, production, and sales were no object?

Russian Imperial Stout

Is there a popular beer you make that you just don't really like but everyone else loves?

Pale Ale

End of a long brew day, what are you drinking?

Mich Ultra. Had a heart attack a few years ago, Doc said no more beer so I switched to Ultra

What are a few beers that other brewers are making that you really find impressive?

DIPA

How do you feel the internet has changed the way the craft brewing industry operates?

Social Media is one of the key ingredients to a breweries success.

When coming out with a new brew, how much experimentation do you try to get in before you say it's ready for production?

None. It is always Go Time here

What style of beer is your bestseller and why do you think that is?

Raspberry Wheat, it appeals to all types of drinkers

Does glassware really make a difference?

Yes in the sense that a $7 beer should not really be in a plastic cup. We have had to for Covid though.

What's the real difference between a Porter and a Stout?

Porter has less punch,

How important is IBU when it comes to picking out a beer? Do customers need to pay attention to it?

"Most" Customers don't really understand but some do We make all of our beers with very low IBU so it pairs with most of our foods

THE POST BREWING COMPANY

105 W. Emma Street,
Lafayette, CO 80026

Brad Landman
Director of Brewing Operations

Typically, how much beer do you guys make in a year?

Around 3,000 bbls per year

How much beer do you personally consume on an average workday?

While working, I really only drink beer from the tanks and taps to make the quality is where it should be. All in, probably 1 beer at work. At home, I usually have a beer or two with dinner. I'm pretty mellow on work days.

What's your favorite food to eat with beer and why?

BBQ ribs are my favorite food in general and they pair very well with almost any beer.

About how much does it cost to open a brewery?

Are you offering? How much do you have? Funny that is exactly how much it costs! Truthfully, it depends on what you want to do. $100k and time looking for used stuff can get you something. $2 million and you can have a great start with lots of upgrades.

What are today's worst beer trends?

I've always liked beer that tastes like beer. I tend to ignore beers that are supposed to taste like something non-beer related. I love German Chocolate cake in cake form. I'm not a fan of it in beer form.

When you first opened the brewery, what was the biggest obstacle? What advice would you give someone thinking about opening a brewery to avoid some pitfalls you experienced?

Cash flow is always an issue. It can take 8 weeks or more from when you brew a beer until you get paid for that beer.

How do you decide on new beers to brew?

We tend to talk them over. At the Post we have always been conservative about brewing beer that follows the trends. Our beer tends to follow the style guidelines.

How did you first discover craft beer and what made you want to enter the business?

When I was underage (in Kalamazoo, MI during the early '90's), I had an older friend who would only buy beer for me if it was craft beer. That always tasted more exciting than the Molson Canadians that I stole from my older brother. When I was 20, I woke up one morning and realized that I could buy the stuff to make beer, just not the beer. We didn't have the internet then, so I went to the homebrew shop at Bell's Brewing and asked a bunch of questions, bought *New Complete Joy of Homebrewing* and some supplies. A few weeks later I had beer and we got drunk on it! Since then I always thought it would be cool to get paid to make beer. Turns out that I was right!

What beer would you brew if cost, production, and sales were no object?

Two of my favorite styles are ESB and Black IPA. The sales on those are terrible, which is sad.

Does glassware really make a difference?

It needs to be clean and hold beer. Ideally it is made out of clear glass. Other than that, it is nice, but not mission critical. I've always subscribed to the "keep beer fun" motto. Having beer in the proper glass is great, but I like drinking beer more than looking at it.

What beer is your brewery best known for and why?

We make a lot of lagers. All our beer is designed to pair with food. Many times the beer is subtle in flavor, but has complexities if you look for them. Other times, you can just drink it and enjoy it for being beer that tastes like beer.

End of a long brew day, what are you drinking?

If I'm being a homer, Howdy Beer is for sure what I'm drinking. I love the flavor and at 4.5% abv, I can drink quite a few of them. It is a very refreshing beer!

Overall, my favorite beer of all time is Bell's Two Hearted Ale. The first time I had it was during college when we went to Bell's 10th Anniversary and they were selling it for 10¢ a glass. I fell in love with it and have loved it ever since. It isn't crazy for me to grab one of those after a long day.

Which hop varieties do you find yourself using most often and why?

I'm old school. I really like the "C" hops (Cascade, Centennial, Chinook, etc). The citrus flavors are great! I've really enjoyed getting to know the Strata hop lately.

What was the first beer you ever brewed and how did it taste?

It was supposed to be a Bock, but with ale yeast. At the time we drank a lot of Huber Bock because it was under $10 out the door for a case in long neck bottles. The beer I brewed tasted something along the lines of Huber Bock. Now that I understand how beer is supposed to taste, it probably sucked. But being able to catch a buzz on something I made that cost less than Huber Bock... Well, that was the best beer in the world as far as I was concerned!

PAREIDOLIA BREWING CO.

712 Cleveland St
Sebastian, FL 32958

Pete Anderson

Typically, how much beer do you guys make in a year?

250-350 bbls per year

How much beer do you personally consume on an average workday?

2-3 pints

What's your favorite food to eat with beer and why?

Tacos , because they're tacos

About how much does it cost to open a brewery

Well in our case our 1st location was small so $50k but bigger breweries we'll over $1million

What are today's worst beer trends?

IMO Pastry Stouts that are sugar bombs

When you first opened the brewery, what was the biggest obstacle? What advice would you give someone thinking about opening a brewery to avoid some pitfalls you experienced?

Biggest obstacle for us was finding a location that worked logistically within our very limited budget. Advice would be to get a very good architect to draw your plans and make friend with people in the building dept.

How do you decide on new beers to brew?

IPAs are a given but we carry a varied selection to cater to as many tastes as possible. Seasonals also dictate to some degree.

How did you first discover craft beer and what made you want to enter the business?

Mid 80s started tryin some new draughts and bottles I'd find around San Diego. Lynn and I talked about opening a pub after moving to Portland OR

What beer would you brew if cost, production, and sales were no object?

Imperial Stout

Does glassware really make a difference?

Yes

What beer is your brewery best known for and why?

Hazy IPA called 32958. We are in the old Post Office and that's our zipcode

End of a long brew day, what are you drinking?

Either a Pale or IPA

Which hop varieties do you find yourself using most often and why?

Citra, Mosaic and Cascade are all in our core brands

What was the first beer you ever brewed and how did it taste?

A Pale Ale and all

I will say is it was drinkable.

PORT O'PINTS BREWING CO.

1215 Northcrest Dr
Crescent City, CA 95531

Rick White
Master Brewer, Veteran, Owner

Typically, how much beer do you guys make in a year?

700 barrels

How much beer do you personally consume on an average workday?

3 pints

What's your favorite food to eat with beer and why?

A good sandwich to complement the beer I drink

About how much does it cost to open a brewery?

$500,000

What are today's worst beer trends?

Glitter, milkshakes, and flavored/fruit

When you first opened the brewery, what was the biggest obstacle? What advice would you give someone thinking about opening a brewery to avoid some pitfalls you experienced?

Local politics, slow TTB processing, water policies. Advice...good business plan, more money than you originally planned, and NEVER GIVE UP!

How do you decide on new beers to brew?

Seasonal weather, holidays, customer input

How did you first discover craft beer and what made you want to enter the business?

Living in Germany and returning to the US where there was few craft beers on the market. I started out as a home brewer and the passion grew from there

What beer would you brew if cost, production, and sales were no object?

Barley wine

Does glassware really make a difference?

Not in our market, it's mostly for "presentation"

What beer is your brewery best known for and why?

Agate Ale - An American Cream Ale...it's the local's favorite - a gateway beer

End of a long brew day, what are you drinking?

Whatever I have on tap at home..usually a witbeir

Which hop varieties do you find yourself using most often and why?

Warrior, Mosaic, Cluster, Cascade, Centennial....to meet the customer's palates

What was the first beer you ever brewed and how did it taste?

American Pale Ale - It was awesome!

PULPIT ROCK BREWING CO.

207 College Dr
Decorah, IA 52101

Scott Nading
Manager

Typically, how much beer do you guys produce in an average year?

1000 bbls

About how much money does it cost to open a brewery?

Depends greatly on size of production, real estate, and taproom design. easily 1 million or more.

In the past few years we have seen a massive surge in the popularity of Hazy IPA's and Sours, what do you believe the next popular beer style will be?

Pastry, pastry, pastry.

When you first opened the brewery, what was the biggest obstacle? What advice would you give someone thinking about opening a brewery to avoid some of the pitfalls you experienced?

It costs much more than you think it does. When you figure a budget, double it.

What beers are you best known for and why?

Pastry sours and stouts. We use REAL ingredients and produce in small batches. This attention to detail and not skimping on the adjuncts leads to a superior product though the profit margins are lower than those who use extracts and concentrates.

What sets your brewery apart from most others?

Dedicated community support. Ex: during the recent pandemic, despite drastically reduced business we donated 10% of all our sales to locally effected business and their employees.

What are the biggest reasons for the continual growth of craft breweries?

Innovation, those places that only brew 'flagship' beers will struggle long-term.

What are the biggest obstacles to continued craft beer growth?

Innovation

What are the biggest problems you run into in producing beer?

Not making enough to satisfy the masses

How do you reach beyond the hardcore beer drinkers and into the general public to sell your beer?

Community support brings many 'novice' drinkers to our establishment that might not otherwise consider trying craft. They hear about the good things we do for our community and want to help support that.

What's the style most fun to brew?

Wild capture/ spontaneous beers

What beer would you brew if cost, production, and sales were no object?

Barrel-aged everything

Is there a popular beer you make that you just don't really like but everyone else loves?

Many

End of a long brew day, what are you drinking?

Good lagers

How do you feel the internet has changed the way the craft brewing industry operates?

Customers are very entitled in this industry. The internet allows them to express their views and opinions directly to the producer as well as their peers. It is a double edged sword as we very much appreciate and depend on the consumer's opinion of our brand and product, but it is often just a lot of whining. Without a doubt the internet creates a massive exposure platform to get your name out there. Good or bad.

When coming out with a new brew, how much experimentation do you try to get in before you say it's ready for production?

Go big or go home. Our brewers are incredibly talented and can work through a new idea on paper and produce a fantastic final product in a commercial batch right out of the gate 95% of the time.

What style of beer is your bestseller and why do you think that is?

Pastry sours, FLAVOR FLAVOR FLAVOR. It is a gateway beer style because it doesn't taste at all like 'beer'

Does glassware really make a difference?

Yes, most importantly a properly CLEAN glass makes a difference, not always the shape or style.

How important is IBU when it comes to picking out a beer? Do customers need to pay attention to it?

IBU is a relative number that is determined during the brewing process, often by the end of a beer that is dry-hopped or dosed with adjuncts etc.. the perceived bitterness is completely different than the stated IBU. We are trending away from even listing IBU as it can limit an uniformed customer from trying a beer that they will ultimately enjoy just because of a number.

POOLES ISLAND BREWING CO.

11695 Crossroads Circle, Suite A
Middle River, MD 21220

Patrick Jones
Head Brewer

Typically, how much beer do you guys produce in an average year?

In our first full year of production we made about 500 bbls.

How much beer do you personally consume on an average workday?

Not as much as I would like. During the shift I consume very small amounts for tasting purposes only. One it's a liability and also I do the majority of the brewhouse work. So getting anything done once you've had a couple of pints is very hard.

What's your favorite food to eat with beer and why?

Spicy tacos with old school West Coast IPAs. The bitterness of the West Coast style can stand up to all that spice.

About how much money does it cost to open a brewery?

It depends on the size but anywhere from $50K for a garage-style brewery to the skys the limit.

What are today's worst beer trends?

That's a loaded question, LOL. There is a lot of creativity in the industry at the moment, and I for one think we should embrace it. Anyone that thumbs their nose at a beer trend in a negative way is just as bad as a beer reviewer that rates a beer badly just because they don't like the style. Even though they said it was a good beer. Not everyone likes the same things. Early on in the craft beer movement it seemed that we had to move mountains to get people to embrace the "new" styles that weren't light lagers. Now are we going to quit at just the classics? Not in my view. If you don't like it, don't drink it. (Dismounts soap box)

In the past few years we have seen a massive surge in the popularity of Hazy IPA's and Sours, what do you believe the next popular beer style will be?

That's the $100,000 question. So I guess it would be based upon what you think the definition of "popular" should be. There are a few styles that are finding a resurgence, usually classic beers like Helles and Pilsner. But i think the direction of real growth for the beer industry will be in products that have a resemblance to beer by incorporating other ingredients as well. Making them taste less like traditional beer. For example, a beer that tastes more like wine or cider. Alternative products so to speak.

When you first opened the brewery, what was the biggest obstacle?

Just building awareness of who and where we are. The popularity of breweries in general these days is enough to spark interest but they won't come if they don't know you exist or can't find you. It's also just a spark of interest. You also have to deliver the goods. People have subjective tastes but quality will ultimately ring true, even amongst the guests with very opinionated palettes.

What advice would you give someone thinking about opening a brewery to avoid some of the pitfalls you experienced?

Back up the money truck. Whatever amount you think you need, double it! I'm dead serious. Even with the garage-style low budget brew kits. You will always need more money than you think. Also, plan on not making any profit for at least a year or more. Budget for that, as well as quality, and you'll be on the right track.

What beers are you best known for and why?

Over the course of my career it would be lagers. I was lucky enough to be a part of small breweries that embraced them. So in the second half of my career I've always kept them in rotation wherever I work. I've won 8 GABF awards and 6 have been for lagers.

What sets your brewery apart from most others?

We embrace the diversity of tastes in our guests. In that spirit, we strive to have something for everyone. Classic styles like Helles, Scottish Ale, West Coast Pale Ale, German Hefeweizen. Trendier beers like Hazy IPAs, Fruited Sours, Barrel Aged Imperial Stouts are almost always on tap. We also like to push the envelope and make cocktail inspired hard seltzer, hard cider, and even beer/wine hybrids that taste more like wine than anything recognizable as beer. Now the ultimate goal is to produce a quality product. Not be a jack of all trades and a master of none.

How do you decide on new beers to brew?

Now that we have been open for just over a year, that decision is a juggling act between what has done well for us in the past and what we think our guests will gravitate towards as a new offering. For example, in the next few weeks I'll be making a non-alcoholic NEIPA. Fingers crossed.

What are the biggest reasons for the continual growth of craft breweries?

With each generation I see a continuation of past successes in this industry. It has grown from unusual and rarely found to commonplace in our daily lives. Craft beer is everywhere. Supermarkets, gas stations, liquor stores, concerts, ballparks, stadiums. It wouldn't be there if people didn't want to drink it.

What are the biggest obstacles to continued craft beer growth?

Quality and saturation. People will drink it if the quality is there, but won't if it isn't. Saturation can and might eventually happen. Too many breweries and not enough drinkers.

What are the biggest problems you run into in producing beer?

QA/QC. It's always been a "what have you done for me lately" issue. You can go from a hero to a goat at the speed of one batch of beer. Most drinkers are more forgiving if you have already won them over. But given enough time with low quality beers they will abandon you for greener pastures.

How do you reach beyond the hardcore beer drinkers and into the general public to sell your beer?

Everything we sell at the moment is via our taproom. So offering an eclectic variety is key in an attempt to win the hearts and minds of the "casual drinker".

How did you first discover craft beer and what made you want to enter the business?

In college I worked at a brewpub in downtown Nashville, TN. Worked my way up to bartender. Eventually after college fell into an assistant brewers position. After a few months I was hooked. Made it a career ever since.

How do you attempt to increase beer production while still staying true to both your brand and your unique styles?

Since we attempt to make such a diverse selection, our brand and unique styles are par for the course. Once the initial honeymoon is over you are no longer the new kid on the block. So an increased marketing effort is needed to increase beer production and subsequently sales. Private tastings, beerfests, etc.

What's the style most fun to brew?

Our beer/wine hybrids. I get to make the most un-beer-like "beer" I can. We combined the very delicately made beer portion to a varietal wine juice (Chardonnay, Sauvignon Blanc, Riesling, etc). Co-fermented with wine yeast, at wine strength, and served still not sparkling. Except for the beer component, I do precisely what a winemaker would do outside of crushing grapes. The end result is almost indistinguishable from wine.

What beer would you brew if cost, production, and sales were no object?

This is a boring response. A North German-style Pilsner. I love the precise control needed to execute such an incredibly difficult style. The window of opportunity with regards to the beer specs is very small. If it's too hoppy, it's out of balance. If it's too malty, it's a Helles. If it's too alcoholic, it's a Bock bier. Also, drinking such a difficult beer to make is extremely satisfying. It's like eating popcorn. You can't put the glass down. Just sip after sip. Before you know it, it's almost empty. Just like eating a bowl of popcorn.

Is there a popular beer you make that you just don't really like but everyone else loves?

The fruited wheat and sour ales. Too much sugar. It gives me a sugar high, like having too much caffeine in a way.

End of a long brew day, what are you drinking?

I drink seasonally, and also it's whatever the mood strikes. Lighter styles in the summer, darker brews in the winter, etc.

What are a few beers that other brewers are making that you really find impressive?

Mixed fermentation beers. We don't make them for the fear of cross contamination. There is obviously a "wild" element to these brews. Some brewers have a deft hand at making these styles, while others throw caution to the wind. I prefer to not drink vinegar.

How do you feel the internet has changed the way the craft brewing industry operates?

Social media has changed it immensely. Some for the good, others for the bad. Review culture has taken a turn for the worse. What could be used as a guide for others, can now be weaponized. Shame.

When coming out with a new brew, how much experimentation do you try to get in before you say it's ready for production?

We have a 15bbl and 2bbl system here at Pooles Island. The 2bbl is precisely for that purpose. Luckily with my experience, a new brew has a higher likelihood of some form of success. It may not be a homerun but at the least it'll be a good representation of what it could be if it does fall short. Usually no more than a couple of iterations. No ones perfect.

What style of beer is your bestseller and why do you think that is?

Hazy IPA. Those styles are far more approachable than the West Coast IPAs. Not everyone is into lots of bitterness, and since they are made to minimize said bitterness that's a plus.

Does glassware really make a difference?

In general it does. Some beers like Hazy IPA can have such a profound aroma to them that the choice of glassware can mute those aromas. So the antithesis of beer appreciation.

What's the real difference between a Porter and a Stout?

Semantics really. The most profound Robust Porter is very similar to the lightest of all traditional Stouts and may be stronger overall in perceived flavor.

How important is IBU when it comes to picking out a beer? Do customers need to pay attention to it?

IBUs can be used as a guide but with the advent of Hazy IPAs it makes it more difficult. A great producer of Hazy IPA with an IBU of 80 (theoretical of course) can taste like 30. But a poor producer of Hazy IPA with an IBU of 80 tastes like a cloudy West Coast IPA. Some will enjoy the former and some the latter. It all depends. Strange times that we live in that a number doesn't always mean what the number says.

CONCLUSION

So after hearing from all these breweries, it's safe to say a few things. First is that somehow they all seem to go all day without drinking beer, perhaps they thought I was a fed. Second is that everyone seems to put their heart and soul into these businesses and unlike almost every other industry, passion, creativity, and quality seem to trump profits. If you have visited as many breweries as I have you will of agree that quality and experience are paramount to the experience. If any of the breweries in this book are in your state, be sure to seek them out and let them know you heard about them in this book.

If you have enjoyed this book, please consider writing a review. It really does make a difference.

IF YOU LOVE CRAFT BEER:
lifelevelupbooks.com/beer

Drink Local and Drink Often

Q&A WITH OVER 300 AMERICAN BREWERIES

A SPECIAL THANKS TO THE FOLLOWING BREWERIES

BOOK 2

- EARTH BREAD + BREWERY
- ELM STREET BREWING CO.
- ESSEX COUNTY BREWING CO
- EIGHT-FOOT BREWING
- ELKTON BREWING CO.
- EAGLEMONK PUB AND BREWERY
- ENID BREWING COMPANY
- ESTES PARK BREWERY
- EDGE CITY BREWERY
- EXPEDINTURE BREWERY
- EAGLE PARK BREWING COMPANY
- ENERGY CITY BREWING
- FIELDS & IVY BREWERY
- FRIENDSHIP BREWING COMPANY
- FOR THE LOVE OF GOD BREWING
- FOULMOUTHED BREWING
- FOUR STACKS BREWING
- FORT SMITH BREWING COMPANY
- FACTOTUM BREWHOUSE
- THE GLASS JUG BEER LAB

- GRINDHAUS BREW LAB
- GATLINBURG BREWING COMPANY
- GIG HARBOR BREWING CO.
- GARRETT'S MILL & BREWING COMPANY
- GLOUCESTER BREWING COMPANY
- GROSSEN BART BREWERY
- GOOD WORD BREWING & PUBLIC HOUSE
- HELIX BREWING CO.
- HILLSBOROUGH VINEYARDS & BREWERY
- HORSE & DRAGON BREWING COMPANY
- HERBIERY BREWING
- HELLBENT BREWING
- HOWLING MUTT BREWING CO.
- HUMBLE ABODE BREWING
- IRON TREE RESTAURANT & FUNKY TOWN BREWERY
- INVENTORS BREWPUB
- JACK PINE BREWERY
- JACKSON STREET BREWING
- KENNAY FARMS DISTILLING
- KNOX COUNTY BREWING CO.
- KELSEY CITY BREWING COMPANY
- KNOTTED ROOT BREWING COMPANY
- KALISPELL BREWING CO.
- KANSAS CITY BIER COMPANY, LLC
- KOI POND BREWING CO.
- LAUNCH PAD BREWERY
- LABYRINTH FORGE BREWING COMPANY
- LAZY BOY BREWING
- LOCUST LANE CRAFT BREWERY
- LOST WORLDS BREWING COMPANY
- LAND-GRANT BREWING COMPANY
- LOCHIEL BREWING
- LONG BREWING
- LOOKOUT BREWING COMPANY
- LIONHEART PUB AND BREWERY
- LANCASTER BREWING CO.
- LENA BREWING COMPANY
- MACKENZIE BREWING COMPANY

- MAUI BREWING CO.
- MADCOW BREWING CO.
- MCALLISTER BREWING COMPANY
- MICKEY FINNS BREWERY
- MOUNTAIN VALLEY BREWING
- MISKATONIC BREWING COMPANY
- MUDDY RIVER FARM BREWERY
- MASH MONKEYS BREWING COMPANY
- MIDDLETON BREWING (MBTX)
- METRIC BREWING COMPANY
- MACON BEER COMPANY
- MISSING FALLS BREWERY
- MOUNTAIN FORK BREWERY
- MODIST BREWING COMPANY
- MT LOWE BREWING COMPANY
- MAD MALTS BREWERY & TAP ROOM
- MAD JACK'S MOUNTAIN BREWERY
- NATURAL STATE BEER COMPANY
- NORTH JETTY BREWING
- NAILERS BREWING COMPANY
- NAKED RIVER BREWING
- NOVEL BREWING COMPANY
- NEXUS BREWERY
- NEWPORT CRAFT BREWING AND DISTILLING
- NORTH FORK BREWING COMPANY
- NEW ENGLAND BREWING CO.
- NECK OF THE WOODS BREWING
- NEW MADISON BREWING
- NEW REALM BREWING
- OLD COAST ALES
- OLD HARBOR BREWERY
- OVERSHORES BREWING CO.
- ON TOUR BREWING CO.
- OPPOSITION BREWING COMPANY
- OLD STOVE BREWING COMPANY
- PARADISE BREWING / PARADISE BREWING SUPPLIES
- PROSPERITY BREWERS
- PESKY PELICAN BREWPUB

- THE POST BREWING COMPANY
- PAREIDOLIA BREWING CO.
- PORT O'PINTS BREWING CO.
- PULPIT ROCK BREWING CO.
- POOLES ISLAND BREWING CO.

Please support the breweries that supported this book!

CPSIA information can be obtained
at www.ICGtesting.com
Printed in the USA
BVHW091428031220
594765BV00010B/1232